1P 1293
7a

Across the Cactus Curtain

The Story of Guantánamo Bay

Across the

Illustrated with photographs, line drawings, and maps

Other Books by Theodore K. Mason

ALL ABOUT THE FROZEN CONTINENT
ON THE ICE IN ANTARCTICA
THE SOUTH POLE PONIES
TWO AGAINST THE ICE: AMUNDSEN & ELLSWORTH

Theodore K. Mason

Cactus Curtain
THE STORY OF GUANTÁNAMO BAY

DODD, MEAD & COMPANY
New York

Illustrations courtesy of: Collection of Theodore K. Mason, 13, 28, 47, 56, 59, 75, 98, 102, 103, 105, 140 *top;* U.S. Navy, by Jerry Lewis, Seaman, U.S. Navy, reprinted, by permission, from *The History of Guantánamo Bay,* U.S. Naval Base, Guantánamo Bay, Cuba, 1953, 132, 136, 139, 142, 144, 145, 146; U.S. Navy, maps taken from U.S. Hydrographic Office charts and local Guantánamo Bay Naval Base Public Works blueprints, reprinted, by permission, from *The History of Guantánamo Bay,* U.S. Naval Base, Guantánamo Bay, Cuba, 1953, 135, 137; U.S. Navy, by permission, 10, 12, 16, 22, 29, 31, 33, 35, 36, 38, 39, 40, 41, 42, 43, 45, 48, 52, 53, 55, 64, 70, 71, 79, 82, 84, 88, 89, 90, 91, 93, 95, 97, 101, 104, 114, 115, 117, 119, 123, 140–141 *bottom;* U.S. Navy, reprinted from *The Daily Gazette,* U.S. Naval Base, Guantánamo Bay, Cuba, 24, 61, 76, 107.

1 2 3 4 5 6 7 8 9 10

Library of Congress Cataloging in Publication Data

Mason, Theodore K.
    Across the cactus curtain.

    Bibliography: p.
    Includes index.
    Summary: Presents an historical account and the
author's personal impressions of Guantánamo Bay Naval
Base, the only United States military base in communist-
controlled territory.
    1. Guantánamo Bay Naval Base (Cuba) [1. Guantánamo Bay
Naval Base (Cuba) 2. Military bases. 3. Cuba] I. Title.
VA68.G8M37 1984   359.7′097291′67   84-13740
ISBN 0-396-08462-1

For Ruth and Graham

Acknowledgments

*T*HE author is grateful to the following for their assistance in compiling the material for this book:

Rosemary Casey, Editor, Dodd, Mead, & Company, Inc.

Anna C. Urband, Office of Information, Department of the Navy

John Coleman, Editor, *All Hands* Magazine

The United States Naval Photographic Center

Angel E. Pinto, Second Secretary, Cuban Interests Section, Embassy of the Czechoslovak Socialist Republic, Washington, D.C.

Peter Hackett, Ruth Walls Books Pty. Ltd, Sydney

and at the United States Naval Base, Guantánamo Bay, Cuba:

Colonel J. B. Hicks, Jr., Commanding Officer, Marine Barracks

Lt. Commander and Mrs. John Pomfrey, United States Naval Reserve

Lt. Commander J. D. Van Sickle, United States Naval Reserve, Public Affairs Officer

7

Lt. Commander H. K. Maynard, United States Naval Reserve, Public Affairs Officer

Captain S. L. Sayko, United States Marine Corps, Intelligence Officer

Captain M. Floryshak, United States Marine Corps, Public Affairs Officer, Marine Barracks

Ensign C. F. McCollom, United States Naval Reserve, Assistant Public Affairs Officer

Lt. Commander D. R. Switzer, United States Naval Reserve, officer in charge of legal services

Lt. Commander S. Brooks, United States Naval Reserve, Intelligence Officer

Photographer's Mate Second Class D. Duguid, United States Navy

Ms. Susan Junkins, Public Affairs Production Assistant

Across the Cactus Curtain

The Story of Guantánamo Bay

Using powerful binoculars, Lance Corporal Eddie Sanchez, U.S.M.C.,
keeps watch over a section of the fence line.

A VC-10 crew arms a TA-4 Skyhawk jet in preparation for participating
in a training exercise.

One

*D**AYBREAK* at Guantánamo Bay, Cuba, finds a small group of United States Marines mustering to enter the world's largest active mine field, 735 deadly acres that have claimed twenty lives since the obstruction was laid down in 1962 during the Cuban Missile Crisis. Fellow Leathernecks on this, the only United States base in Communist territory, have also rolled out. They're getting ready to relieve other Marines who have maintained a vigilance during the previous watch in the lookouts and on patrol along the 17.4-mile fence line that isolates the naval facility from the rest of the island.

Across the bay at the Leeward Point airfield, Navy pilots of the only "operational-ready air strike squadron" in the Caribbean are on 24-hour readiness to defend the base from attack. In that event, the squadron with its Sidewinder missiles, bombs, and rockets would be joined on the ground by four hundred Marines, two rifle companies of Navy men, five M-60 tanks, machine guns, artillery, and mortars. Although hopelessly outnumbered, they would try to hang tough until help could arrive from the United States and other Caribbean bases.

Ironically, each morning also finds Cuban dayworkers riding buses from nearby towns to work on the base. Most of these *guasanos*, or worms, as they are chastised by Cuban-government supporters,

Cuban dayworkers leave the base through the Northeast Gate to return to their homes.

have been up since 4:00 A.M. When they arrive at the "Cactus Curtain," they will be searched by the Cuban militia and forced to change clothes before walking along a mile-long "cattle chute" across no-man's-land to the Northeast Gate. After passing through the checkpoint, the commuters will exchange identity cards and board buses for their jobs in the shipyard and repair shops.

It's one of the anomalies of this, the oldest United States base on foreign soil, that workers from an avowed adversary are employed where almost all of the Atlantic Fleet is trained. No other Cubans (or anyone) can visit this "restricted facility" without permission, and no base personnel can cross the closed frontier into Cuba.

As the tropical sun climbs higher in the sky, the six thousand base residents stir from their beds to begin another day. Military personnel, civil servants, Cuban exiles, and Jamaican contract workers prepare to start work. Wives get the kids ready for school before facing the daily challenge of shopping at the commissary and Navy Exchange.

Oblivious to their precarious situation, the denizens assume each new day will be another routine, if not boring, one at Gitmo, as they call this outpost of America. But as Gitmo alumni know, the prevailing atmosphere of tranquility and nonchalance is not guaranteed. It has been scrambled periodically by hurricanes and political storms since the Spanish-American War, when Cuba, grateful for its independence, agreed to lease the reserve to the United States for as long as its North American neighbor wanted the area. The annual rent was put at only two thousand dollars. Although inflation has increased the sum to $4,085, it is still the world's biggest military bargain.

By contrast, the United States in 1983 renewed its agreement with the Philippines to lease two bases in that former colony at 900 million dollars each for five years. Cuban President Fidel Castro might be envious, and economically unwise, if Cuba wasn't compensated by the Russians. (For a look at Gitmo's history, see Appendix A.)

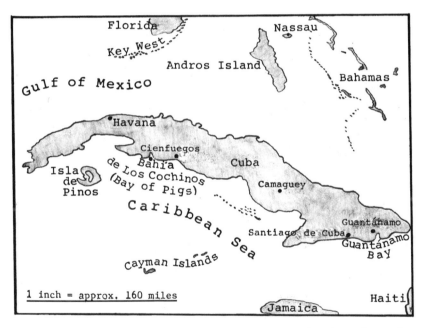

Guantánamo Bay, 500 miles southeast of Miami, Florida, is located in Cuba's Oriente Province.

In the early days, the Marines periodically used Gitmo as a staging point on their way to help quell rebellions in Cuba and on other Caribbean islands. But there was no direct threat to the base until the late 1950's when Castro began his bid to wrestle power from President Fulgencio Batista, a harsh and corrupt dictator. Batista, who had seized control in 1952 with the backing of the United States, had been supplied with munitions from Gitmo, although this was prohibited by treaty.

On June 27, 1958, rebel forces fighting in the Sierra Maestra Mountains near the base kidnapped twenty-nine sailors and Marines who were returning to Gitmo from liberty. The insurgents, who were led by Raúl Castro, Fidel's brother, held the servicemen as hostages in the hills until releasing them through diplomatic channels on July 18.

The United States, as would be expected, declared Cuban territory off limits. The Marines increased their posts along the fence line and refined their security procedures.

Castro succeeded in toppling Batista in January of 1959, when Batista fled to the Dominican Republic. The frontier was closed, forcing thousands of Cuban workers to walk through the Northeast Gate to work instead of driving into the base. (Some also continued to arrive by ferry until 1962.)

With Gitmo's fate hanging in the balance, relations between Castro and the United States began to deteriorate as the new Cuban leader initiated a program of sweeping economic and social changes. In a direct challenge to the United States, his government started confiscating private property, much of which was owned by North Americans. He sent agents to initiate revolutions in several Latin American countries, and he established close ties with Communist countries, particularly the Soviet Union. Promising to defend Cuba, the Russians replaced the United States as Cuba's primary trading partner and source of financial support and military supplies.

At the same time, Castro vociferously continued to denounce the United States and accuse his powerful neighbor of trying to undermine his government. In March of 1960, when a French ship carrying arms from Belgium to Cuba exploded in Havana Harbor, killing seventy, Castro accused the United States of sabotage. The United States denied any responsibility.

As relations continued to deteriorate, Congress passed legislation enabling President Dwight D. Eisenhower to cut the quota of sugar purchased from Cuba. Soon thereafter, the United States placed an embargo on all exports to Cuba except food and medicine. Castro retaliated by accelerating the confiscation of North American property. In total, over one billion dollars in United-States-owned interests were taken, for the most part without compensation.

Castro also condemned the North American presence at Gitmo and accused the United States Embassy staff in Havana of paying counterrevolutionaries to plant bombs in his country. He demanded that the U.S. reduce its embassy staff from eighty-seven to eleven within forty-eight hours. As a further punishment, he prohibited any additional hiring of Cuban workers for Gitmo.

Most Americans at that time believed Castro's charges were the paranoiac ravings of a deranged mind. In 1975, however, it was revealed that the Central Intelligence Agency had indeed trained thousands of Cuban exiles in a whole bag of dirty tricks, including poisoning crops, sabotaging factories, and hijacking Cuban planes and ships.

The assassinations that the C.I.A. attempted to arrange included Castro's. The agency also hatched a plot to make his beard fall out and, in May of 1960, began preparing exiles to invade the island. It is believed that the Cuban government knew of this invasion scheme, as did some American newsmen and others.

Nevertheless, President Eisenhower, in one of his last acts in office, severed diplomatic ties with Cuba on January 3, 1961, in response to Castro's ordered reduction of the embassy staff.

The new United States administration of John F. Kennedy decided, after much debate, to continue with the C.I.A.'s invasion project. It was a disaster. The twelve hundred anti-Castro exiles (some sources put the figure slightly higher) landed at the Bay of Pigs on the southwestern coast of Cuba on April 17. The 1112 survivors were captured and imprisoned. (They were eventually ran-

Nopalea, predominate type of cactus in the "Cactus Curtain"

somed and returned to the United States between 1962 and 1965.)

During the Bay of Pigs fiasco, rumors of retaliation against Gitmo invaded the base, several hundred miles to the southeast. Castro, however, made no threatening moves, although he had his militia plant eight miles of cactus along the northeastern section of the fence line during the fall of 1961, physically creating what had already been symbolically established as the Cactus Curtain to stop Cubans from using the base as a conduit for escape.

By its failure in and embarrassment from the Bay of Pigs invasion, the United States created the impression that it wouldn't use the necessary force to back its opposition to the Castro regime. Assuming this, Soviet Chairman Nikita Khrushchev believed the United States wouldn't take steps to prevent the installation of Soviet ballistic missiles in Cuba, which he had promised to defend with Soviet arms.

He dangerously miscalculated. After United States U-2 spy planes flying over the island detected a ballistic missile on a launching site, President Kennedy announced a naval "quarantine" of the island. (He carefully avoided using the term "blockade," which is an act of war, as did President Ronald Reagan in July of 1983 when he ordered a quarantine of Nicaragua.) Kennedy warned that United States Forces would seize any offensive weapons and associated material that Soviet vessels might attempt to deliver to Cuba.

At Gitmo, meanwhile, the CO (Commanding Officer) had called a routine DEFEX (Defense Mobilization Exercise), the sixth of the year, for Sunday, October 20. Suddenly, with Kennedy's startling announcement, the mobilization was no longer an exercise.

Base leaders learned only an hour beforehand that the Marines of the First and Second Marine divisions were on their way to reinforce the local defenders. The abrupt arrival of so many men presented some logistical problems, including how to feed them. But Gitmo managed. Many hot meals were replaced by 3500 sandwiches that were turned out each day.

Heavy rains, the first precipitation in six weeks, drenched the Marines in their field positions. To alleviate this miserable situation, a clothing store on wheels was improvised. Later, shuttles relayed the Marines to showers for temporary relief from the sun and dust.

At 10:00 A.M. on the day after the Marines landed, Gitmo's CO announced the evacuation of dependents and civil servants who wanted to leave. Many housewives had the Monday wash on the line. He told them they should pack one suitcase each and take important documents. They were to tie pets in the yard, leave keys on the dining table, and stand in front of their houses and wait for a bus to pick them up. Since then, dependents have been required to keep a suitcase of essentials packed in case of evacuation.

Buses took 2777 dependents and civilians from the Windward side of the bay to the piers. They boarded four ships and were underway by 5:00 P.M. Meanwhile, planes began evacuating dependents from the Leeward Point area, hospital patients, and expectant mothers. During a seventy-hour period, 188 four-engine planes arrived and departed from the airfield.

The only women who remained on the base were ten Navy nurses and one Red Cross representative.

On board the ships, problems with berthing and feeding had to be overcome. Winter clothing was highlined from a fifth ship to replace the tropical clothes most of the evacuees were wearing. When they arrived at Little Creek, Virginia, residents from the Tidewater area flocked to greet them and brought clothing, food, and offers of lodging.

Back at Gitmo, the Seabees and the Marines began building new roads and hundreds of reinforced concrete bunkers through the hills. Security guards were ordered to protect housing areas that had been emptied for tactical reasons.

After a week during which the United States prepared for war, Khrushchev informed Kennedy (October 28) that work on missile construction sites would be stopped. Missiles already in Cuba would be returned to the Soviet Union. Satisfied by continued reports from U-2 flights, the United States lifted its quarantine on November 20. Castro, however, was furious, and threatened to shoot down the planes. But Khrushchev, who was famous in his own right for temper tantrums, wisely told the Cuban to cool it. Castro had no recourse, although he attempted to salvage his pride by refusing to cash the annual rent checks for Gitmo.

Signs of the subsiding threat began to appear at Gitmo soon after talks finished between the Super Powers. Football season opened with the Naval Hospital defeating the Seabees 30–12. Off-duty Marines could be seen teeing off on the golf course, where their tents added to the sand trap hazards.

But it was the return of dependents that signaled the situation had returned to normal. The first group arrived by plane on December 7, with the understanding that they might have to pack up and leave again. Perry Como, who was making a personal appearance at Gitmo, was one of those on hand to greet them. The reinforcing Marines left four days later.

By Christmas, most of the families had returned. Reunited with husbands and fathers, they were treated to Ed Sullivan's 1962 Christmas Show, which was taped on the base.

During the Missile Crisis, as in the case of the Bay of Pigs invasion, base residents were relieved that Castro didn't strike back at Gitmo by shutting off the water.

For years the lack of fresh water was a primary drawback to the development of Gitmo as a fleet operating base. In the early days, water had to be purchased on a yearly contract from Guantánamo City. Tank cars transported the vital cargo to Caimanera and Boquerón; from there Navy barges delivered it to the station, and it was pumped into storage tanks. This method was costly, unreliable, and dangerous to the health of the residents. Attempts including well borings, catchment reservoirs, and a distillation plant failed to secure a water supply on the base.

In 1934, Congress had authorized the Navy to contract for water from the Yateras River, ten miles north of the base, and five years later the water began flowing to two treatment plants on the base. Stored in three steel tanks, two million gallons of water was used daily.

A small additional water supply was added early in 1963 when eight productive wells, drilled near the existing Cuzco Well, were hooked up to one of the water plants.

The water situation appeared secure, even through the threatening times with the Castro regime. But on February 6, 1964, Castro accused the United States of stealing water and turned it off. The charge, of course, was ridiculous. Castro actually was furious at the United States for arresting thirty Cuban fishermen who had been caught in four boats fishing illegally in territorial waters off the Florida coast. Although the fishermen had been returned unharmed to Cuba, Castro decided to teach the United States a lesson. Cutting off the water, however, was like shooting himself in the foot. It deprived him of all economic benefits of the base, particularly the payment of fourteen thousand dollars a month for the water.

With only fourteen million gallons of water stored on the base, Gitmo faced the most serious threat in its history. The Navy ordered strict water conservation. Water for home use was rationed to a one-hour period three times a day. Laundries, dry cleaning, lawn watering, and all nonessential uses were prohibited. The seven swimming pools were closed. As Gitmo began drying up, water barges were dispatched from Jamaica and tankers from Florida. A converted T-2 tanker was towed to the base and used to store water.

During the Water Crisis, Gitmo's commanding officer, Rear Admiral John D. Bulkeley, joined the Marines on the hill overlooking the Northeast Gate. Dressed in battle greens and packing his "Big Iron," a 3.57 Colt magnum pistol, on his hip, Bulkeley stood watch for twelve to eighteen hours a day.

A survey team arrived from Washington and reported to President Lyndon B. Johnson, who decreed that Gitmo would become as self-sufficient as possible. This meant building a distillation plant and dismissing Cuban employees. Two hundred fifty Cuban workers were fired on February 12 and escorted off the base. Eventually more than two thousand of the innocent Cubans were retrenched. To replace them, additional Navy personnel were ordered to the base and seven hundred male Jamaicans were hired. Castro, as a result of the changeover, lost most of the $7.8 million that the commuters took into the Cuban economy each year.

At the same time, the Chief of Naval Personnel announced that no additional dependents would be permitted to go to Gitmo, which was being put on garrison status. Dependents already on the base could remain only until their tour was scheduled to end.

By February 17, Bulkeley, who had rescued General Douglas MacArthur and his troops from the Philippines during World War II, had taken enough of Castro's blackmail. He ordered his men to cut the two pipelines used to carry the water to the base and remove a section to disprove the Cuban accusation. While the admiral and fourteen United States journalists observed, a 38-inch, 300-pound section of the 14-inch pipe and a 20-inch section of the 10-inch pipe were severed and lifted from the ground. The openings were then sealed permanently.

To no one's surprise, the insides of the pipes were dry.

Cuban harassment of the Marines on fence-line duty increased after the pipelines were cut, apparently to provoke an incident. For months before, Cuban guards had taunted the Marines by throwing rocks and making obscene gestures.

Persisting in its harassment, the Cuban government complained to the United States that the Marines had destroyed the property around the Cuban guardhouse at the Northeast Gate. They accused the Marines of using abusive language and actions which degraded their guards. They claimed the Marines had taken down the Cuban flag, thrown it on the ground, and used provocative action against the guards on Cuban territory.

To expose these lies, Bulkeley stationed a team of Navy motion picture photographers on what became Bulkeley Hill to photograph all activity at the gate. The Cubans in return tried to blind the cameras with large spotlights. Not to be defeated, Bulkeley ordered the Seabees to construct a thirty-foot circular slab of concrete on the hillside and paint the Marine Corps emblem on it. His countermove worked. Not wanting to herald the Marine Corps, the Cubans turned off their lights.

Action was also taken to eliminate the rock throwing and other abuse by the Cubans. Marine guard posts were moved back from the fence line; although the Cubans started using slingshots, they were unable to stone the Yankees effectively. Cut-off roads were constructed to keep the Marines at a safe distance from the Cuban guards, who would come along the fence at night and pelt American vehicles on patrol.

Meantime, a sea water conversion plant at San Diego had been dismantled and transported to Gitmo, while construction started on a plant at Fisherman's Point to convert sea water and produce electricity.

The Cuban Government in mid-July leveled a more serious charge against the Marines on the fence line, accusing a Marine sentry of firing several shots that killed one of the Cuban guards. But, according to the Marine, he had been fired on first and, when he fired back, he aimed a single bullet over the heads of the Cuban guards, who were 250 yards away. Immediately after the shooting, an ambulance, photographer, and several Cuban guards arrived on the scene, which was at a remote area along the fence line. Since normally it would have taken them forty-five minutes to reach the

Gitmo's desalination and power plant

spot, the Navy decided the shooting had been a carefully planned incident.

A few days later, Castro announced that he was pulling back his 450 men to keep them from being killed by the Marines.

The Navy had an announcement of its own. The desalination plant had been reassembled and was ready to go. Selecting July 26—the Cuban equivalent of the Fourth of July—as the inaugural date, the plant began producing 750,000 gallons of fresh water daily.

When Mrs. Bulkeley turned the valve to start the water flowing again, the swimming pools reopened. The Navy allowed limited watering of whatever lawn and shrubbery hadn't dried up and changed the uniform of the day from dungarees to whites.

A couple of weeks later, twenty pieces of Cuban earth-moving equipment began clearing an area of about two hundred yards on the Cuban side of the fence. Along with clearing the trees, cacti, and underbrush, the Cubans constructed a new type of pillbox that included escape trenches with concrete sides and tops. They put up a zigzag barbed-wire fence that varies in distance from two-and-one-half miles to within one hundred yards of the American barrier. They also moved out of the guardhouse at the Northeast Gate.

On September 7, the second unit of the water conversion plant became operational, adding another 750,000 gallons daily to the base water supply. No longer needed, the last of the two tankers that had been bringing water from Florida ended its run. The tankers had brought in 293 million gallons of water during the crisis.

A third desalination unit was on line by December. Indicating that Gitmo had returned to normal, the Chief of Naval Operations announced on Christmas Eve that families would be allowed to come to the base once again. The Navy also gave its okay for base residents to wash their cars, disguised by nearly eleven months of Gitmo dust.

Since the Water Crisis, Gitmo has nearly become the self-sufficient installation that President Johnson intended. A fourth boiler and fresh water evaporator have been added, giving Gitmo's desalination plant a capacity of three million gallons daily. Because of the high cost of fuel needed to operate the boilers, however, only 1.2 million gallons of water are currently produced each day.

Lawn watering is permitted only one-half hour each day; at other times, residents are encouraged to save dirty dish water to sprinkle their patches of green. Washing cars is similarly limited to certain hours.

The same turbine generators that are used in the transformation of salt water provide daily 248,484 kilowatt hours of electricity at a daily cost of $33,063. Before the plant was installed, all electrical power was generated in power plants on the base. Only a limited amount was purchased from Cuban plants until October of 1961, when floods damaged the transmission lines. The Cuban Government claimed to have made the necessary repairs, but the power supply was never resumed.

As in the case with water, electricity consumption is conserved as much as possible. Air-conditioners are not allowed to be turned on until 1:00 P.M., and then only if the temperature rises above

Energy Tip of the Day

```
Flush  the  commode  only  when
necessary, and never for dispos-
ing of scrap paper,  cigarettes,
gum wrappers,  etc.  Each flush
uses about 3.5 gallons of water;
make     each     flush     count.
```

The Daily Gazette publishes energy tips as part of the campaign to conserve energy.

85° F. Street lights go off between 1:00 A.M. and 5:00 A.M.

To ensure that such rules are obeyed, a small, full-time Energy Team seeks out energy waste. Energy-saving tips and the daily energy use are publicized to make residents aware of their performance. With the endless bombardment of "save energy" campaigns, conservation instead of fleet training often seems Gitmo's primary mission. The conservation efforts, however, have literally paid off. In 1982, over one million dollars was saved and used to pay for new furniture in the Gold Hill Barracks and for new street curbing.

The Energy Team also looks for water waste and coordinates with Gitmo's Port Services to prevent oil waste by visiting ships.

As these measures suggest, Gitmo has settled down to its own special daily routine, since the two great crises of the 1960's. But it is an uneasy tropical tranquility, threatened by the tremors of Caribbean tensions and international politics.

Two

GITMO stands today as the last symbol of the former neocolonial relationship between Cuba and the United States. As such, it is an infuriating symbol that sticks in the craw of Fidel Castro. In his 1962 speech on the anniversary of his revolution, Castro damned the base as "a dagger plunged into the Cuban soil." While he pledged not to remove the base by force, he vowed that "it is a piece of land we will never give up." Since 1962, he has repeatedly called for the return of the territory, as did the Non-aligned Nations at their summit conferences in 1964 and 1976.

Some United States politicians also have joined the "return Gitmo" chorus, including former senator and presidential candidate George McGovern. Had he instead of Richard Nixon been elected, the United States probably would not have a naval base in Cuba.

For Castro, the question of Gitmo is not open to negotiation. He has ruled out anything short of complete withdrawal from Gitmo as one of the five steps toward normalizing relations with the United States. He claims that the United States illegally occupies Guantánamo. Since his government didn't sign the treaty, it is not bound to respect it, in his opinion. He also contends that the treaty isn't valid because it was imposed on Cuba—a contention that is incorporated in the Cuban constitution as Article 10.

Although Castro is right about the conditions under which the treaty was enacted, he is, according to most experts in international law, stuck with the situation because he promised during the early days of his regime to honor all international obligations. He could ignore international law and attack Gitmo, but this would provide the U.S. with the justification of invading Cuba and removing him.

His only persuasive legal argument is not universally accepted in the world community. In this view, when conditions prevailing at the time a treaty was signed have drastically changed, the treaty should be considered no longer valid. Such was the legal basis for the turning over of the Panama Canal to the Republic of Panama by the United States. But the United States is not about to listen to the same justification from Cuba, simply because, unlike the canal, the United States has little to gain from sacrificing Gitmo. Faced by increased Panamanian hostility over the canal's sovereignty, the United States bowed to the wishes of Panama in the interest of preserving good relations and continued use of Panama by the U.S. Armed Forces.

In addition to his argument that the United States illegally occupies Gitmo, Castro contends that the base would be dangerous to Cuba's welfare in the event of a war between the United States and the Soviet Union. That may be so, but Cuba faces a much greater risk from the increased Russian military presence in Cuba and from the use of the island as a distribution center for revolutionaries and for Soviet-block weapons destined for Latin America.

In his television address to the nation on March 24, 1983, President Reagan displayed reconnaissance photographs of increased Russian activity in Cuba, including the expansion of the intelligence collection facility at Lourdes, "the largest of its kind in the world," only one hundred miles from the U.S. mainland. It is manned by fifteen hundred Soviet technicians.

President Reagan showed another aerial photo, this one of a military airfield in western Cuba where MIG-23 and antisubmarine warfare planes are stationed.

Reagan's report added to intelligence previously released, revealing that the Russians had increased the number of their infantry combat brigade from 2600 to 4300 on the island. (President Jimmy Carter had insisted that the Russians remove this brigade and staged a Marine Reinforcement Exercise at Gitmo as a show of force, but the Russians ignored the demand.) It has also been known for some time that the Russians have stationed several warships, including submarines, in Cuba on occasion.

In his address, Reagan also warned that the level of Russian arms exports to Cuba "can only be compared to the levels reached during the Cuban missile crisis twenty years ago." He displayed photographic evidence showing large amounts of Russian military hardware in Nicaragua, and he questioned the purpose of the airfield construction in Grenada. He termed the Soviet-Cuban militarization of Grenada a "power projection into the region through which much more than half of all American oil imports now pass. . . ." The region is also important, he stressed, because it is an area where the United States is trying to help several governments in their "struggles for democracy" against guerrillas supported by Cuba.

Less than seven months later, the Marines invaded Grenada. Some sixty Cubans working there were captured or killed. Among other things, this should demonstrate to Castro that his actions rather than the presence of Gitmo are more likely to draw fire.

A third reason why Castro wants the United States out of Guantánamo Bay is because he fears the U.S. might provoke an incident there to justify an American invasion of Cuba. And he has manufactured facts to support this contention. According to figures published by the Cuban Ministry of Foreign Affairs, there have been 12,668 incidents by the U.S. Armed Forces at Gitmo during the period 1959–1979. These incidents include 6606 violations of Cuban air space, 1303 violations of Cuban waters, and 5300 acts of provocation, including shooting (and in some cases, killing) Cuban sentries on the fence line.

Despite all of Castro's impassioned rhetoric, some reporters have surmised that he isn't anxious to have Gitmo back. According to this conjecture, if Gitmo were returned, the Russians, who currently spend $11.5 million a day in economic aid to support Cuba, would insist on becoming the new tenants at Guantánamo Bay.

Also, it helps to bolster a dictatorial regime like Castro's to have such a convenient whipping boy as the United States and its Cuban base.

Whatever Castro's actual feelings about Gitmo, his arguments have not convinced the United States to abandon it. The Navy doesn't want to lose its "Gibraltar of the Caribbean." And in the Navy's estimation, the importance of Gitmo has increased rather than diminished. The Navy insists Gitmo is a vital link in the defense strategy of the United States.

Along with the naval bases at Key West, Florida, and Roosevelt Roads, Puerto Rico, Gitmo dominates the main maritime entrances to the Caribbean and the Gulf of Mexico. The hundreds of islands and thousands of square miles there would be difficult to patrol without Gitmo. From Gitmo, the Navy also protects the safety of the air routes from the east coast of the United States to the west coast of South America and guards the security of the approaches to the Panama Canal.

More than its strategic value, its usefulness makes Gitmo important. From its Gibraltar-like position, the Navy can provide search and rescue assistance, antisubmarine warfare support, aircraft ser-

Anti-Air Warfare Center atop John Paul Jones Hill, Gitmo's highest point at 494 feet. Leeward Point airfield is in background.

vices, and disaster relief for neighboring islands. A Coast Guard aviation unit handles the search and rescue operation. The Coast Guard detachment also helps with the program to intercept boatfuls of Haitian refugees and the efforts of the United States Drug Enforcement Agency to catch drug traffickers in the busy Gulf of Mexico corridor. Gitmo is also the only overseas Shore Intermediate Maintenance Activity (SIMA), which is Navy jargon for a shipyard, including dry dock, that can handle all but major repairs.

But Gitmo is valued most as a naval facility for training the crews of the Atlantic Fleet and some allied navies. Its location provides perfect weather conditions that permit shakedown and refresher training throughout the year. It has a big, land-locked bay sheltered from the weather. A 100-fathom curve lies at the mouth of the bay, enabling the largest ships to begin deep-water training within minutes of weighing anchor.

The fourteen thousand square miles of training area to the south are free of major air and sea traffic, allowing freedom of movement to ships, aircraft, and submarines. At Norfolk, Virginia, by contrast, it takes six hours or more for ships to clear sea traffic. Gitmo offers the necessary isolation for gunnery and antisubmarine warfare practice, too. And its offshore waters are perfect for sonar training.

Gitmo is also attractive for training because shore leave can be controlled easily without the diversions found at most ports.

Some have argued, however, that, even as a training facility, Gitmo is replaceable. They contend that nearby Roosevelt Roads Naval Base duplicates most of Gitmo's functions at much less cost and with less potential international confrontation. But, according to the Navy Department, there is no duplication. The Puerto Rican facility, which has four ocean training ranges, can conduct multiship training exercises, whereas Gitmo is basically set up to train one ship at a time.

The Navy concedes that "it is technically feasible to relocate. . . ." But the cost to relocate, including increased costs for ship transit time and for delays in meeting schedules, "would be considerable."

U.S.S. *Stark* passes Leeward Point on its way to sea for training.

A different justification for Gitmo is its political and psychological importance. This argument maintains that the base stands as a symbol of United States power, prestige, and purpose in Latin America, particularly in view of Castro's dedication to exporting Marxist revolution. The Castro threat has acted recently to quiet those who question the strategic value of Gitmo in view of the technological advances in modern weapons, although some critics still maintain that the cost of operating Gitmo is too much to pay for a symbol.

In 1977 the Secretary of the Navy proposed closing Gitmo. Although his recommendation was reversed, the facility was "consolidated." Two officers with the rank of captain replaced the admiral who had previously served as commanding officer, and there was an overall reduction in personnel of 30 percent.

Gitmo also has a potential political use as a "bargaining chip" in the pocket of the United States. In this capacity, the base could be used to win concessions from either Cuba or the Soviet Union. For example, Ambassador to the United Nations Adlai Stevenson urged President Kennedy during the Missile Crisis to consider offering Gitmo in exchange for the removal of the Russian weapons if the

31

quarantine of Cuba failed. In Stevenson's opinion, the base was not strategic to the defense of the United States.

Along this same line, it is possible that one day the United States will surrender Gitmo in a good will gesture as part of a move to normalize relations with Cuba. But that sunrise appears further away today than ever before. The Defense Department announced in 1984 that it plans on spending $43.4 million to improve the base, the greatest investment in Gitmo since World War II.

Some news reporters, after a rare, government-conducted visit to the base, have echoed the opinion that the United States isn't getting its money worth out of Gitmo. They have tagged the base a "28,000-acre amusement park" and "a paradise for alcoholics and sports lovers among the Navy's 'lifers.' " Not so, argues the Navy, citing the long workdays put in by most of the servicemen.

Any evaluation of Gitmo, it seems, depends on who is asked and the state of Cuban-United States relations at the time.

Those who have served a tour of duty at Gitmo are just as divided in their opinion of the place. To some, Gitmo is a Caribbean paradise; to others it is a penal colony. Approximately 80 percent of married personnel extend their duty to stay on; bachelors usually count the days until they leave, although some (who risk being accused of having "rock fever") volunteer for tour extensions. A few have even retired at Gitmo, although current base policy prohibits it.

What's the attraction? For one thing, a Gitmo assignment for enlisted personnel counts against the time they have to spend at sea. They also receive the extra bonus of sea pay. All personnel can save money because there's little at Gitmo to spend money on. Further, there's little crime. The warm, sunny weather enables residents to enjoy an outdoor life. And Gitmo's location offers the chance to travel in the Caribbean.

But even for those who enjoy Gitmo, life on the Rock isn't paradise. They agree it is a frustrating, isolated experience, like living on an island within an island. It's also similar to a small town where anyone's business is too often everyone's business.

Despite the controversy surrounding it, most Americans have

never heard of Gitmo, or at least don't know much about it. I was among this majority when I was assigned there as a Navy journalist. I was as amazed as if I had been told the Russians had set up camp in Alaska. How was it possible? More to the point, wouldn't it be a dangerous place for me to be?

Nobody at Pensacola, Florida, where I was stationed at the time, could tell me much about the place, although my executive officer insisted it wasn't any duty for me. He made it sound like one of the armpits of the world: "You don't want to waste your time spinning records at Gitmo," he assured me and said he was requesting an extension of my present tour.

I was appreciative, even flattered, though I didn't understand why the exec thought Gitmo wasn't for me. Duty in the Caribbean seemed appealing. It conjured up gloriously sunny days; balmy nights; warm, aquamarine water caressing coral reefs; mother-of-pearl beaches dressed with gracious palm trees. What could be so undesirable about Gitmo and duty with the Armed Forces Radio and Television Service (AFRTS)?

By refusing my extension at Pensacola, the Bureau of Naval Personnel gave me the chance to find out, as it does hundreds of other lucky service personnel every year.

Cuzco Beach, for base personnel only, is a protected reserve. The U.S. Naval Cemetery, upper right, is one of five in the world.

Three

*B*EFORE. leaving their duty stations, those destined for Gitmo have to be inoculated and obtain permission for any dependents to follow them when housing is available, which is usually in ten to twelve months. Those who want their families to join them must stay for two years; others only have to serve a twelve-month stint.

It's a difficult decision for married personnel, but most opt to have their families with them, even if it means they will be together for only half of their Gitmo tour. Visits by dependents or other guests are expensive and limited to thirty days. Visitors are allowed only if housing can be found for them, either at the home of a host or one of the transient quarters. Sponsors must also pay the cost of the round trip ticket.

One inducement to bring the family (and serve the extra year) is that living in a house is more comfortable than in the barracks, unless one doesn't care about such things as privacy, home-cooked meals, personal belongings, pets, and a car.

Having neither dependents nor pets, all I had to do was pack my sea bag and report to the Norfolk Naval Air Station. Twice a week, American personnel, priority supplies (including fresh vegetables), and mail are flown from Norfolk to Guantánamo Bay. The job is handled by either MAC (the Military Airlift Command of the United

States Air Force) or a chartered civilian airline, which I took.

After several hours of flying south over the dark blue Atlantic, the captain announced that we had skirted the island of Cuba and were preparing to approach the base.

"We're not allowed to fly over Cuba. You need a U-2 for that!" he said with a laugh.

The Cuban Government, to the contrary, claims that the United States repeatedly violates its airspace when flying into and out of Gitmo, and is not amused.

As our jet began to drop, I joined the necks of the uninitiated, craning for first impressions of our new duty station.

"There it is, folks," the captain's voice proclaimed. "Those of you on the right side of the aircraft can see an East German cargo ship steaming right through the middle of our base! You won't see that anywhere else in the world. Forty miles north, in the mountains, is Guantánamo City, center of a region producing coffee and sugar . . . and Russian MIG's!"

To the dismay of the stewardesses, those of us who weren't returning residents unbuckled our seat belts and stood up to get a better look.

Soviet merchant ships and those of other Communist nations are often seen passing through the harbor to Cuban ports in the upper part of the bay.

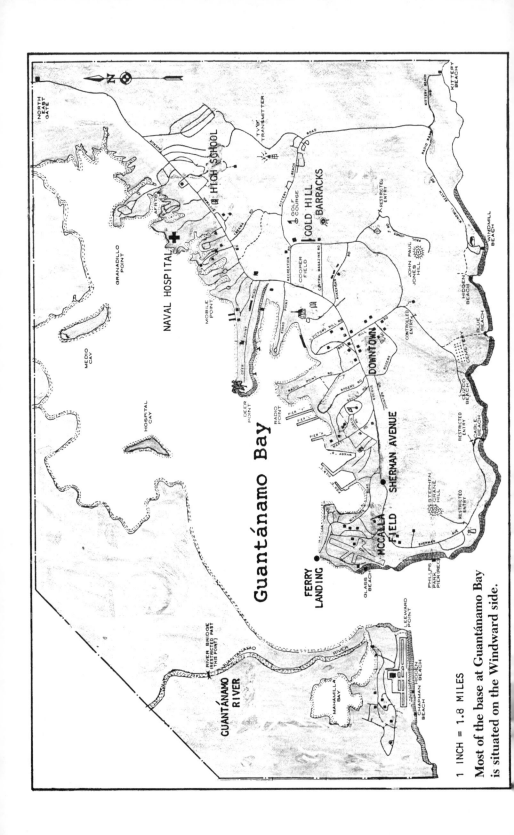

Guantánamo Bay

1 INCH = 1.8 MILES

Most of the base at Guantánamo Bay
is situated on the Windward side.

A quick scan of the area revealed that Guantánamo Bay was not what I expected. Unlike other parts of Cuba, this region of Oriente Province isn't characterized by lush vegetation. Only swatches of green can be seen among the parched brown hills and the inlets of the bay which, four miles wide and twelve miles long, represents 30 percent of the base area.

Discovered by Christopher Columbus, who was searching for riches and found none, the bay divides the base into east and west sectors, the Leeward and Windward sides. Two airfields straddle the narrow entrance to what is possibly the most zealously and expensively guarded harbor in the world.

Yet there is nothing threatening or dangerous in the appearance of the base. Seen from the air, Gitmo could be an inconsequential port town. The fence line, lookout towers, minefield, and the armed vigilance aren't visible.

Our plane quickly swooped down and began braking on the 8000-foot runway of the Leeward Point airfield. The cabin seemed to burst into chaos as the passengers competed to get off with their children, carry-on bags bulging with goods not always available at the Navy Exchange: cosmetics, children's shoes, casual clothes, and just about anything that can be crammed into a bag, including house plants.

When I stepped from the air-conditioned cabin, the heat and humidity, not oppressive but enough to make me sweat in my wool dress blues, rushed to greet me. A woman on the plane had told me to expect weather comparable to San Diego, which didn't endear Gitmo to me. I was put through boot camp in San Diego.

For other people, however, both places have appealing climates. Gitmo's is characterized by warm, sunny days, occasionally interrupted by rain showers and thunderstorms. Nearly one-fourth of the total average annual precipitation of twenty-four inches falls during October. The temperature ranges from 80° to 90° F. Because it's located in the belt of trade winds, the base is refreshed by a sea breeze from the southeast during the afternoons; a few hours after sunset the wind backs to a northerly direction and becomes a land breeze. However, mountains that encircle the base

37

to the west, north, and east act to shelter the base, producing less precipitation and a larger temperature range than on the windward side.

Walking toward the MAC terminal, I reconnoitered the scene for clues to my fate. Departing passengers, fearful of missing the return flight, it seemed, mobbed the doorway of the terminal, where louvered windows appeared gasping to catch the sea breeze. Three small buses, painted the Navy's favorite color (gray), waited to take us to the ferry as two flatbed trucks moved in to unload our luggage. Fortunately for my first impression, I couldn't see the fence line, three-quarters of a mile away.

Parked near the hangers, several Skyhawks of Fleet Composite Squadron Ten (VC-10) stood ready to launch at a moment's notice. Although equipped with an arsenal of weapons, they are no match for the MIG-23 fighter-bombers stationed at the former United States airfield at Los Caños, thirty miles north near Guantánamo City. The MIG-23's, which can be configured to carry nuclear weapons, fly three times the speed of sound, easily outmaneuvering the Skyhawks. As an indication of their obsolescence, there are only "several" Navy squadrons still flying Skyhawk jets. This fact suggests the United States doesn't consider the base to be in any danger, despite how much Castro insists he wants it back. (The Department of the Navy has declined to address questions concerning the squadron's defensive effectiveness.)

The VC-10 home, once called "Hungry Point" because of the lack of messing facilities, today is an almost self-contained air sta-

The Military Airlift Command terminal handles nearly all passengers and air cargo.

Located at the airfield are an elisted barracks complex (top of picture), a Navy Exchange and mini-mart (lower left), and the Leeward Lyceum (center).

tion. Everything is provided to reduce the need of commuting across the bay to "Mainside," as the Windward sector is called on most bases. The Leeward Point facilities include quarters for officers and enlisteds, a mini-mart shop with ice cream parlor, Navy Exchange, outdoor movie theatre, galley, legal office, fish-and-gear locker, recreation area, and, as if to confirm its development, a police headquarters. Leeward residents have to cross the bay only to take the kids to school, to do serious shopping, and to attend scheduled social events. Gertrude Stein might have called Leeward Point an island within an island within an island.

Leaving the airfield, our bus bumped down a short, serpentine road to the Leeward Point ferry landing. Boatswain's mates herded us, together with some airfield workers and their cars and motorcycles, onto the boat, a converted landing craft (XLCU). Nicknamed *Lucy, Charlie Brown, Linus,* and *Snoopy*—what could provide better evidence that Gitmo is an outpost of America?—the ferries went into service in 1970. The XLCU's were overhauled to double the carload capacity and speed of Gitmo's 1943-vintage ferries. The antiques were sold to the Paraguayan Navy, which didn't seem to mind that they were painstakingly slow.

A Gitmo ferry shuttles passengers and vehicles between the Windward and Leeward sides of the base.

Some of *Snoopy*'s sun-blistered crew wore the traditional Navy dungarees. Others had on khaki walking shorts and white T-shirts— the forerunner of Calvin Klein's "active wear." Knee-length, the big, baggy shorts reminded me of the tropical uniform worn by soldiers in Africa and Asia during World War II.

I wondered as I boarded the ferry (and more so when I wore the shorts myself) why the Navy hadn't sold the uniform to Paraguay along with the old boats.

Once loaded, *Snoopy* maneuvered and chugged through the choppy water toward Fisherman's Point, the large, hook-shaped tip of the Windward side. The passengers were suddenly quiet, their attention focused on the approaching lighthouse. Built in 1903, it was manned by the Coast Guard until the late 1950's, when an automated light was placed on the hill behind it and a second light put on the Leeward side.

As we neared the ferry landing, McCalla Field, an officer's housing area, and the desalination and power plant greeted us. The airstrip, laid out on the south side of historic McCalla Hill, was built in 1931 to accommodate dirigibles, and later, seaplanes. Today, McCalla is no longer used except by helicopters from visiting ships and as a backup in the event of an emergency. Although its runway of five thousand feet is too short for jets, it is perfect for drag racing, sounds of which split the air every Sunday.

After our two-mile transit, which the Peanuts Gang make every half hour, *Snoopy* bumped against the small pier. Once the crew had guided the cars and motorcycles off, the passengers were turned loose and rushed into the clamorous crowd waiting to board or greet returning residents.

Among the parked cars I spotted some crazy-looking contraptions. These, I found out, were Gitmo Specials, a common sight on the base. Specials are older cars that have been modified with abandoned parts scavenged from the base metal scrap yard, known to the locals as Sears. No credit cards accepted, of course.

All such Specials must have bumpers, lights, windshield wipers, key ignitions, and mufflers. The rest is left to the imagination, and there's no lack of that. Some look like experimental vehicles from the past; others resemble chunks of heavy furniture on wheels.

Despite their popularity, these inventive cars aren't a threat to Detroit. They can't be taken off the island. But they do enjoy a long life at Gitmo, being passed on from one happy owner to the next, although not everyone appreciates them. "I wouldn't be caught dead riding in that chest of drawers," is a frequent comment. Children who are sensitive about their image don't like being picked up from school in one.

The main threat to the longevity of the Specials and cars in gen-

A Gitmo Special, displayed
by its owner, Floyd Hokes

eral is the coral dust. It chews up auto parts and it's hard on auto paint. To help those who battle to save their vehicles, Gitmo's Special Services opened a hobby shop in 1975 at a cost of $52,730. The Navy Exchange Auto Repair Shop also carries parts for minor repair needs. Parts that must be ordered can take from six weeks to three months to arrive.

Because of the corrosion factor, many people when assigned to Gitmo don't ship cars that are new. On the other hand, personnel are advised to bring only models less than six years old because of the lack of repair parts. If this isn't enough to encourage drivers to switch to motorcycles or mopeds, then the high price of gas will.

Those who decide to leave their cars behind can rent a car, motorcycle, or moped from Special Services. Or, they can rely on taxis, which run until midnight on weekdays. There's a free bus service, too, for those who don't plan to be out after midnight.

Similar buses had been arranged to take those of us tagged as "unaccompanied enlisted" (which always made me feel as though I had a repugnant social disease) to our "unaccompanied enlisted

The U.S.S. *Nicholson* (982), a destroyer, and the U.S.S. *Kilauea*, an ammunition ship, moored at two of Gitmo's five piers.

An example of Gitmo's family residential sites

personnel housing," more commonly called the barracks.

Leaving the airfield, we climbed a small hill and discovered in the distance a Navy destroyer berthed at one of the piers just beyond "Downtown" Gitmo.

The bus quickly dropped down into a group of concrete block houses, box shaped, their harshness softened somewhat by patches of lawn, a few flowering bushes, and the occasional palm or rubber tree.

The lack of imagination can be attributed at least in part to the amount of money available to build the units, which were put up in the 1950's as two, three, or four family units for enlisteds. (Officers, as on other bases, enjoy single units, which usually have more room and better landscaping.)

There are eighteen roughly similar residential areas for military personnel with accompanying families. There is also one each for Jamaican workers and Cuban refugees.

Although not of the most intriguing architecture, the houses are considered hurricane proof, a necessity during the June-November season. Concrete-slab roofs and reinforced glass or metal louvered windows distinguish the hurricane-proof houses from the wood frame structures that date from the early 1900's.

The newest houses on the base are a result of the construction boom of the 1970's when Gitmo got a considerable face-lift. In April of 1973, 150 three- and four-bedroom townhouses for married enlisted personnel were completed. At the same time, remodeling and repairs were done to improve the older concrete block houses, and many of the hazardous wooden structures were torn down.

As the bus trundled on, we continued past the familiar motor pool in a reclaimed salt flat between two promontories probing the bay. Just beyond, brown pelicans soared and strafed. It was encouraging to see my high-school mascot at Gitmo. The presence of this endangered species made Gitmo seem less foreign, less threatening.

Our bus lurched as we struggled up the next hill. The driver, a smiling, gap-toothed Jamaican, fumbled with the gears. At the top, we poised, overlooking Downtown. The bus faltered as the driver, his soaked shirt pinned to his shoulder blades, worked the bedeviled gears.

His impatient passengers shouted advice and abuse.

"Put it in first!"

Suddenly the bus lurched and, with the advice-givers clutching seat backs, we bolted down the hill. We careened through the intersection, nearly sideswiping a truck and a Gitmo Special full of teenagers waiting at the only stoplight on the base.

THIS IS A STOPLIGHT! protested the sign hanging from the signal.

The frantic driver wheeled desperately into the commissary parking lot, where the bus smacked into the rear bumpers of two parked cars.

Leaping out the door, the driver fled among the cars broiling in the afternoon sun. Shoppers flocked around while we piled out and stood a safe distance away, eyeing the vehicle as though it might have been involved in voodoo.

"You could have been killed!" a woman shopper assured us.

The police arrived immediately in a gray, unmarked pickup. Dressed in short-sleeved khakis without rank or insignia and wearing white helmets, two young men got out and began asking questions.

44

Downtown Gitmo at the intersection of Sherman Avenue and Bay Hill Road

Gitmo's police force is made up of Navy personnel specially recruited and screened for the job. In addition to the police force, the traditional shore patrol is used to maintain order at social and recreational events. Members are picked from the various departments on the base and from visiting ships with people ashore on liberty.

I never found out what happened to the driver. Presumably he didn't attempt the long swim home and eventually returned to his quarters. All civilians, both U.S. and non-U.S. citizens, are subject to prosecution under Title 18 of the United States Code for any serious crimes committed on the base. Offenders normally would be prosecuted by the United States Attorney in the Norfolk Federal District Court, since Norfolk is usually the port of entry for those returning to the States from Gitmo.

This legal precedent was set in 1965 after a bizarre murder case. A Cuban named Pellicier chased an unarmed Jamaican named Scott across the athletic fields and whacked him to death with a machete.

45

The murder created a legal problem because Pellicier was a Cuban national who had committed a crime on a U.S. military base. Although Cuban civil law applies to Gitmo, the U.S. doesn't recognize it, and there is no other civil law on the base. On the other hand, Pellicier couldn't be tried in the United States since Gitmo was not within the jurisdiction of any Federal District Court.

The Navy Judge Advocate General and the United States Attorney General reasoned that the base lies within the "special and maritime and territorial jurisdiction of the United States" and this special jurisdiction applies to all base residents.

Under heavy guard, Pellicier was flown to Miami. He was indicted for murder, but before the trial began he was found incompetent.

Less serious legal matters are up to the CO, who has the power to revoke the offender's "privilege" to reside at Gitmo. Because such a decision would result in loss of employment and possibly family separation, the accused is usually given ample opportunity to rebut the alleged charges. In such cases, Gitmo's judge advocate holds an informal hearing prior to the CO's decision.

Military members, as they are on any other United States base, are subject to court-martial prosecution under the Uniform Code of Military Justice.

While the police were concluding their investigation, a replacement bus arrived and took us to the barracks. When we arrived at our new home, we unloaded and stood gawking at the swimming pool in the sun-scorched courtyard. Was the pool intended for us or had it been placed there to appease the humanitarian demands of the International Red Cross and the Geneva Convention?

"Hey! Will you take a look at that?"

"We must be in the wrong place!"

"Maybe we died and went to heaven."

"More likely the other place. The chow smells like the same old crap."

Suddenly a voice boomed like a wrathful god angry at the criticism of his creation. "What are you turkeys gawkin' at? Get your tails over here!"

46

Enlisted Navy men were billeted at Bay Hill Barracks, 1942-1970. The pool was a welcome sight to new arrivals.

Like a shot we were back in the Navy. The MAA (master-at-arms), who was one of the authentic old salts of the Navy, stood in the doorway, his beer belly protruding between T-shirt and skivvies. Puffy faced and red eyed, he looked angry for being rudely awakened from his siesta.

We hustled and lined up in front of his office where we received our bedding—two sheets and a pillow case—and a locker key. The MAA, whom everyone called Pops, warned us about bed check at 2200 hours (10:00 P.M.) and told us to report to him in the morning for the job of policing around the barracks. We were to be saddled with the task of picking up trash until we had been processed by personnel for our assigned duty.

Moaning under our breath, we trooped off to our cubicles.

From the two made-up mattresses on the two double bunks, I discovered I shared my cubicle with two other sailors. I set my linen on the available top bunk, its mattress sagging like a ski run for cockroaches. At such moments in the service, I thought what I wanted most was a firm mattress.

Life for unaccompanied personnel at Gitmo has improved significantly since then, however. The new Gold Hill Towers barracks,

47

Built in 1970 to replace Bay Hill Barracks, Gold Hill Towers, the Windward Unaccompanied Enlisted Personnel Housing, accommodates 800 Navy enlisted men and women.

built on a hill overlooking the athletic fields, accommodates about eight hundred enlisted Navy men and women. Despite the sound of its official name, Unaccompanied Enlisted Personnel Housing (UEPH), the barracks is a vast improvement over the old Bay Hill Barracks, built during World War II.

The Towers consist of three reinforced concrete buildings, three-stories high, which are supposed to withstand the perils of hurricane, fire, and earthquake. The quarters are air-conditioned and have three lobbies and recreation rooms. But probably the biggest difference between the old and new quarters is the presence of women.

Enlisted personnel are assigned according to their rank and their sex. Chief petty officers get their own rooms, whereas first and second class petty officers must share with a roommate and use a communal bathroom. Third class petty officers are assigned three to a room. Women and civilians are similarly billeted in a separate section.

During the building of the Gold Hill facility, the construction workers found a message inside each carton of windows received from a manufacturer in Miami. "Made by Cuban Refugees, Miami—

God Bless you all at Guantánamo Bay," read the message, written in pencil on yellow tablet paper.

Other military groups also have been blessed with new quarters. Unaccompanied officers have motel-style, air-conditioned rooms with private bath, a mess, lounge, and recreation area.

Not to be left out, the Marines got a new barracks in 1975 to replace the one destroyed by fire the previous year. The Marines' UEPH has 164 rooms that can accommodate 492, with individual baths and air-conditioning.

Despite all of the recent construction at Gitmo, though, housing remains in short supply. Married personnel arriving with their families often have to stay temporarily in the Navy Lodge, Gitmo's hotel/motel, which was opened on September 10, 1983. (Visiting guests and civilians can also receive authorization to use the 26-room facility.)

The housing shortage is a story as old as Gitmo itself. During the early years, commandants of the base lived aboard a ship stationed in the bay. One of the popular tales of housing hardship relates how in 1939 an officer was forced to live in a thatch-roofed house when he reported for duty.

Housing and other major building programs have prospered during periods of war (1917-1919, 1941-1944, 1951-1953, 1969-1975), which prodded the United States Government into providing money for badly needed construction and maintenance. But the result of this sporadic feast-or-famine policy is that the base is spread over 19,625 acres of land and lacks a continuity in layout. Some projects have never been completed, such as the one-million-gallon water storage tank on Commandant's Hill, started in 1904.

Four

*T*HE morning after my arrival, one of the MAA's "runners" found me sweating in the hot sun while I plucked trash from the desiccated weeds and clumps of brown grass on the hillside near the barracks.

"Pops wants to see you," the sailor sneered, his voice suggesting I had done something to deserve contempt.

I followed him in trepidation to the quarterdeck area of the barracks (the entrance hall). There, the impatient MAA waited with a tall, unkempt young sailor who looked as if he'd just jumped out of bed, slapping on his white hat on the way. It was creased and pushed down on his forehead exactly as we'd been admonished in boot camp never to do. His wrinkled khaki shorts suggested he had worn them for several days; his scuffed shoes looked as though he had pursued saboteurs on a search-and-destroy mission through the Gitmo hills. Because the summer uniform (T-shirt and shorts) bore no insignia, I couldn't be sure of his rank or job specialty.

"Looks like you're gonna be one of the Wigby boys." Pops screwed up his hound-dog face, making this distinction appear as appetizing as the poached powdered eggs we'd been served that morning in the mess hall.

"Wrong!" corrected the brazen young sailor. "We're officially AFRTS now. No more WGBY. Gone is the Voice of the Windward

Passage. Another fine Gitmo tradition down the tube. Sorry about that, Pops."

The MAA glared speechlessly at the sailor's insolence, his face flushed as he retreated to his office where his authority remained unassailable.

Sizing me up, my peer said in his normal voice, "You must be the new JO. Chiefy Poo sent me to fetch you to the station. I'm John. We're on a first name basis at the station, though the chief has ruled against it. Familiarity undermines discipline, he says. It breeds contempt. And he should know what he's talking about! Come on, I've got the truck."

Behind the barracks we climbed into a gray pickup with AFRTS stenciled in blue on the doors and tailgate, which John had parked in the space marked MAA ONLY.

As we squealed away, Pops watched furiously from his office window.

John took the prohibited one-lane fire road down the hill, passing the Barrel Club where Jamaicans cleaned up from the night before. Between the imported Royal Palms guarding both sides of Sherman Avenue, we turned onto the main highway, which runs like a backbone through the Windward side of Gitmo.

John revealed that he, like me, was a JO (journalist) with the rank of second class petty officer. Quickly he fired point-blank: "Are you a DINFOS graduate?"

I confessed that I hadn't been to the Information School run by the DOD (Department of Defense). The Navy had designated me a journalist because of my civilian newspaper experience. But I had never been inside a TV or radio station.

"Terrific!" He laughed sarcastically, rolling up his impish blue eyes. But then he attempted to reassure me, saying, "Don't look so worried. All of the crew has been trained on the job . . . as any of our viewers can tell."

While we zoomed on, exceeding the base speed limit of 35 mph, I listened to his caustic commentary of the AFRTS affiliate and Gitmo in general. He delighted in giving me the impression I was about to join the AFRTS counterpart of *M*A*S*H*.

The W. T. Sampson Elementary School, with amphitheater

Overtaking a gray van, he explained, "That's our cattle car. It's used to take the fleet sailors back to their ship at night when the clubs close. They pack 'em in there like livestock." Dropping his head back, he bellowed, "Moo-oo-oo!" and laughed, enjoying the effect on me.

I smiled pleasantly, as if accustomed to people bellowing every day of the week, and began studying the landscape.

Retrieving my attention, he pointed out the chapel and the W.T. Sampson Elementary School on the hill overlooking Cooper Field, Gitmo's athletic area. The elementary school was built in 1975 to replace the several buildings and quonset huts that had served as temporary classroom facilities. Named for the Spanish-American war admiral who headed the United States Fleet in Cuban waters, the $3.6-million school can accommodate 725 students, including kindergarten tots.

The school operates much like those in the States. Bus service is provided for kindergartners and for the older students who live more than one mile away. Students are expected to bring their lunch or snack and are urged to keep a chemical coolant in their lunch box because of the hot weather.

Further up the highway, John pointed out the junior-senior high school, which had 325 teenagers enrolled. This "institution for military brats," as he called it, is fully credited and differs from other junior-senior high schools primarily in its lack of a cafeteria. Students may bring lunch, eat in the enlisted galley down the road, or buy something from the Navy Exchange Mobile Canteen, which stops on the school grounds at midday.

The students wear much the same type of clothing as their coun-

Above: The W. T. Sampson High School. *Below:* Near the high school, this chapel provides Catholic and Protestant services. Other chapels serve Pentecostal, Mormon, and Church of Christ groups.

terparts elsewhere: jeans and T-shirts. But there are some notable taboos in the Gitmo dress code. Prohibited are athletic apparel, thongs, tank tops, short blouses, halter tops, tube tops, short shorts, and clothing such as T-shirts that display "indecency," or advocate drugs or "national dishonor"—in short, most of what kids like to wear.

It may not be any consolation for Gitmo's teenagers, but an equally dim view is taken of such clothing on the other side of the fence. For such a clothing crime, a Marine guard at the United States Interests Section in Havana was ordered in 1983 to leave Cuba within twenty-four hours. He had been turned in for wearing a T-shirt emblazoned with "Cuba yes, Fidel no" to the beach and while putting out the garbage. Nations must be wary of the power of T-shirts.

Seventy teachers are contracted each year to try to teach Gitmo's students. Before the first WAVES arrived in 1972, the teachers and nurses represented the only potential dates for Gitmo's unmarried men.

Being one of those bachelors, John was quick to point out the quarters of the women teachers overlooking the golf course.

"Off limits," he cautioned. "You stand a better chance with the nurses. If you get caught in their . . . quarters . . . you can claim you were looking for the corpsmen's quarters. They live next door over there at the hospital." He flagged his thumb toward the two-story complex, its windows gleaming like squares of burnished copper in the morning sun, beside the bay on Caravella Point.

A reinforced concrete building, the 102-bed hospital was the first fully air-conditioned Navy hospital when it was built in 1956. As a short-term treatment center, it provides medical service for base residents, visiting ships' crews, and United States diplomatic staff and their families from Haiti and Jamaica. The hospital has its own repair shops and morgue as well as quarters for the nurses and enlisted corpsmen.

Gitmo also has a dental clinic, now located at McCalla Field. Navy dentists handle service personnel and their dependents, and a dentist comes from Jamaica every two weeks to care for civil ser-

The Naval hospital

vice employees, Cuban exiles, and Jamaican contract workers.

Beyond the hospital, we passed the zoo and enlisted swimming pool at Deer Park. After turning left, we crossed a dry flat of cactus and weeds where the AFRTS building mushroomed like an oversized, menacing bunker on the bay's muddy shore. (Today, this deserted area has been transformed into an enlisted housing area.) I realized as we neared the single story structure that it was joined by a covered walk to a similar windowless, concrete block building.

"That's the Morin Center next door," John said when we parked in front of the AFRTS side. "It's the Navy's idea of a perfect night out on the town: dinner, drinks, and some worn old Spanish dolls stomping around the stage."

Named for William H. Morin, a boatswain's mate second class who was awarded the Congressional Medal of Honor for disabling twenty-seven mines in the bay during the Spanish-American War, the facility was built as a community center and restaurant in 1962. Two years later, it was remodeled to accommodate AFRTS and *The Daily Gazette*, Gitmo's six days a week newspaper. It is currently occupied by the Fleet Reserve Association and open only to members, who can join the FRA for fifteen dollars a year. Only snacks

The author in front of the AFRTS building, which also housed *The Daily Gazette*

and beverages are served. The Knights of Columbus and Cub Scouts also use the facility as a meeting place.

John opened the glass door to the AFRTS half of the complex, greeted the pretty receptionist (an officer's wife), and led me to the smoke-polluted office of the chief petty officer. Left in command of the station while the officer-in-charge was on an extended trip off the Rock, the veteran Navy JO sat at an executive desk, dramatically flanked by the American and Navy flags. He wore neat, tropical khakis and puffed a large, foul-smelling cigar.

To John's obvious astonishment, the chief got up and shook my hand, saying warmly, "Welcome aboard. Sit down."

He returned to his chair, positioned my personnel file in front of him, took out a lined yellow tablet and ball point, and moved the ashtray, affixed with the Navy emblem, closer to him. Then, with cigar in hand, he began asking questions about my background and experience in the Navy. John stood, disdainfully, leaning against the partition behind me.

The chief concluded the interview with the startling announcement that he was transferring John to the news department and, in spite of my lack of broadcast knowledge, placing me in charge of the television operation. I was to supervise the crew and arrange the program schedule.

My eyes were beginning to tear from the cigar smoke, which appeared to create the impression I was greatly moved.

The chief smiled his appreciation, saying, "I think part of our problem is that John got too close to the crew. Maybe someone new can get them squared away. They know their job, but they need someone to make sure they do it. I can't be here day and night to supervise what's going on. I have a family—"

Someone in the next office snorted and coughed. "You'd have more time at home, chief, if you spent less time on the golf course."

"Shut your trap, Ski," the chief warned, turning angrily toward the partition of rippled green fiber glass that separated the offices.

A bulbous nose on a hair-fringed head with two lopsided blue eyes twinkling like the devil's emerged at the top of the partition.

"A little exercise wouldn't hurt *you*, you know, Ski," the chief suggested in a paternal tone as he tried to recover his smile.

"Whenever I feel the urge, I lie down until it passes."

"Okay, Ski, that's enough. Get to work."

The yeoman first class disappeared like a jinni commanded back into his bottle, although he continued chuckling just loudly enough to irritate his boss.

The chief appointed John as my sponsor, ordering him to take me around the base and get me checked in at the required departments, then to begin my TV instruction.

Scowling, John made no attempt to disguise his attitude.

"You're not upset, are you?" the chief asked, a smile toying with the corners of his mouth. "I thought you'd be happy to have another assignment. Consider it a lateral promotion."

"Peachy."

"Good. I wouldn't want to create any discontent among my men." The chief smirked.

On the other side of the partition, Ski began choking.

"You'd better get started," the chief concluded.

"Aye, aye, Chief," John sounded off. Snapping to attention, he clicked his heels and marched off with his reluctant apprentice in tow.

When we were out of earshot down the hallway that forms a contiguous wall with the Morin Center, I made a feeble attempt to tell him I was sorry about what had happened.

"Don't be," he said with an unconvincing wave of his hand. "I'm glad for the change."

Through a padded door, we entered the television studio. Behind the first of two large control-room windows, the radio DJ watched us curiously.

"That's Guber, God's representative at Gitmo. He's so good-natured it's sickening. He actually believes that hog-wash about offering the other cheek." Turning toward the window, John shouted some traditional Navy obscenities.

Thinking he was being introduced to me, Guber beamed and lifted one side of his earphones to indicate he couldn't hear what John was saying.

Guber, as I was to learn, served as one of several DJs at the affiliate, which has an AM station that plays contemporary music twenty-four hours a day, an FM stereo music station, and a channel broadcasting news from a direct news link with AFRTS in Washington, D.C.

The TV station, which began broadcasting on December 24, 1955, as the first one in the Navy, was upgraded in 1970 to become the first all-color TV facility in the Navy. In 1980, Channel 8 began receiving satellite service from the Alaskan Forces Satellite Network for live sports, news, and special events. As a result, programming is comparable to that of the major United States networks. Although Cuban television from Santiago de Cuba can also be picked up on the base, it provides little viewing competition except for the reruns of old American cartoons, which give Gitmo aficionados a chance to watch such vintage characters as the original Mickey Mouse.

Beginning my crash training course, John turned on the studio working lights. I tried to relate my stage lighting experience from college in an attempt to appear a little less hopeless.

But John wasn't impressed. "We don't try to get creative. We just turn on the lights and trust they'll do the job. There are other more important things to worry about," he said, swinging one of the two cameras around on its wheels.

"These babies are as obsolete as our foreign policy. They're down half the time. But other than that little detail, they're not difficult to operate. Just point and focus."

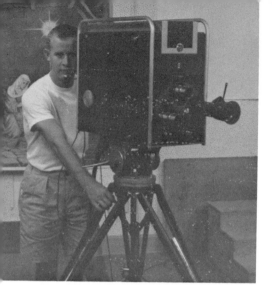

The author tries one of the television cameras.

He promised to demonstrate the camera operation during the nightly hour of live programming: news in English and Spanish, followed by one of several local entertainment shows. That evening featured *Command Quiz,* a weekly quiz program in which teams from two of the base military units sparred for the prizeless championship.

"Tonight the Public Works Department takes on the Nurses in the quarter finals," John informed me, adding with a grin, "We tried to get them to appear in swimsuits, but they declined. Claimed it was inappropriate. Now, I ask you: what could be more appropriate than increased viewer ratings?"

He moved toward a green felt-covered table, where the event would be staged.

"The show can be difficult for the director—that's you—especially when the moderator announces the wrong answers and the phones start ringing. All of us are required to submit the questions and answers each week. But some jokers around here aren't very diligent about checking the correctness of the answers." A grin implied he hadn't always resisted that temptation as he added, "It provides much-needed comic relief, though Chiefy Poo fails to see the humor."

He showed me through another padded door to the television

control room, with its panel of intimidating instruments before a large window.

In the adjoining projection room, he explained the two projectors, used to feed filmed programs into the transmitting equipment.

Next to the projectors, boxes of 35-mm films were lined up on the cement floor. "Every week a shipment arrives with almost enough programs for one week of broadcasting. If you're lucky, there'll be some musical or comedy specials that you can repeat to fill the gaps. AFRTS thinks we're using material from our film library in the attic," he said, pointing to the acoustic tile ceiling above our heads. "Mausoleum would be a more adequate description. Everything up there is as useless as a dead body, which AFRTS should know if they ever read their inventory lists. Just think of it as a challenge."

As John plunged on, I understood my job would involve fitting the films together like pieces of a puzzle into a weekly schedule resembling what Gitmo residents had been accustomed to in the States.

"You're free to change the schedule I've made, but I suggest you don't screw around with the programming too much or you'll have an uprising on your hands. As Chiefy Poo likes to brag, we're the only source of news and entertainment for this small American outpost. Heaven forbid!"

He took me next through the side doors into the heat outside and back into the refrigeration of the station. There, in the rear of the building, he showed me the newspaper production area, although in his broadcasting-biased opinion the Gitmo *Gazette* didn't rate very high: "Not fit to wrap fish."

Published five days a week, the Navy's only "daily" shore-based newspaper features national and international news along with Navy and local news. Each Friday the staff put out a supplement, *The Entertainer*, a four-page schedule of movies, TV programs, and upcoming special events at the clubs.

In a small, doorless office alongside the newspaper area, a balding Puerto Rican man was consuming a cigar the size of a small log while he poured over pages of teletype. Cigars, it seemed, were a

THE DAILY
GAZETTE
Guantanamo Bay, Cuba

The Daily Gazette provides Gitmo residents with a four-paged, 11" x 17" newspaper every day except Sunday.

symbol of status and authority, but I hoped I wouldn't have to smoke one to establish my position.

"That's our Don Alfredo. They say he was hired as translator for the admiral, but the Old Man didn't have any need to *hablé español*, so they dumped him out here. He co-hosts the lunchtime radio show with Guber. Can you imagine that combination on the air? We ought to call it the international comedy hour. Our *don* also broadcasts both radio and TV news in Spanish. But the more we deny being Radio Free Cuba, the more I'm convinced he isn't here as any reject. He's probably working for the National Security Agency monitoring events in Cuba."

Wondering how much of this was a sea story, I watched as the subject extracted his cigar daintily with two fingers and peered at his viewers as though facing a TV camera. Like a good trooper, he flashed a beaming smile.

"What's he smoking?"

"He claims the best Havana. But it smells more like some of the local weed to me."

John led me over to the large aluminum coffee urn outside the newsroom door. He tapped it for two cups, saying, "If Castro don't get ya, Ed's poison will. Teaching our Hey-mon anything is a challenge. Last week he drove the truck into the bay and nearly drowned poor Chiefy Poo. Since then, he's been maintaining a very low profile. And our would-be leader has given up any pretensions of having his own chauffeur."

In the newsroom, John's new assignment, two desks faced each other and two filing cabinets stood next to a panel of radio-receiving equipment for the nearby teletype machines. The receiver

61

emitted a soft, steady electronic beep as though counting Cuban cosmic rays. John lifted the long roll of yellow paper spilling out of one of the machines and scanned the latest Associated Press report.

"Be careful this doesn't get you into trouble," he mused, patting the teletype affectionately on the side. He elaborated that we were supposed to use only the AFRTS-edited news received daily at the communications center. News from the wire service was intended for the admiral's morning brief. Like the admiral, the JO's didn't care for the AFRTS version, which was tailored to its military audience and twenty-four hours old. They often used the wire service news instead. "Every once in awhile someone catches us using news AFRTS didn't report and it all hits the fan."

Ski suddenly peered around the door frame and giggled, "Bubble, bubble. Caldron churn, turmoil and trouble!"

"Come on," John told me, "let's get out of here before it catches."

Ski crept behind us as we walked up the hallway to the front of the building. John grabbed the pickup keys from the board of hooks on the wall, and we swept out the door.

With his disappointed fleshy face pressed against the glass, Ski watched us drive toward Sherman Avenue.

"Don't pay any attention to Ski," John cautioned. "He may seem to have Rock Fever, but it's all an act. At least, I think so. He gets away with murder by acting outrageous. He knows the chief won't put him on report because it would demonstrate a lack of leadership. That's what keeps me off the carpet, too—as long as I don't go too far. The chief's hustlin' to get recommended for warrant officer. With the lieutenant away, this is his big chance to prove his stuff. That's why he's taken over the morning brief . . . and put you in as supervisor."

The reminder stabbed me, as he added, "The chief knows the lieutenant can't stomach him—probably because they're so much alike. The lieutenant wouldn't recommend him for Gitmo Pound Master, which is the smartest thing that hot dog's ever done— besides staying away for months at a time. When both of them are here, it's like the Spanish Inquisition."

John continued his briefing while he shepherded me around the base to the offices of the various facilities and services required by the check-in ritual: medical/dental, recreation, Red Cross, chaplain, post office, library, personnel, and so on. Our final stop was the commanding officer's welcome aboard indoctrination.

John guided the pickup into a parking space marked OFFICERS ONLY and with a grin told me where to go.

I entered the building and followed his instructions to a classroom on the ground floor. It was stifling and hot in the airless room. Taking a seat in the back, I joined the sweating group of sailors and Marines.

A first class petty officer soon marched in and shouted, "Attention on deck!"

We new arrivals stood stiffly at attention as the captain strode in: a crew-cut, immaculate man with rows of impressive ribbons above his left pocket and a circled star, the sign of command, pinned to the middle of the other pocket of his starched-to-death tropical whites. He stepped up to the dais and, after a quick survey of his audience, began:

"Berlin has the wall; we have the fence. Like Berlin, we are unique, an outpost of freedom. Because of our special situation, you will be asked to endure more than normal conditions would require."

He enumerated the salient Gitmo regulations, recreational activities, educational opportunities, and reminded us to write home. Division petty officers, he told us, would be checking to ensure that we kept in touch with family and relatives.

Mail call, as he suggested, is an important weekly event at Gitmo because it helps residents to feel less isolated. Mail, which takes from three to nine days to reach the base, follows no set schedule, since it depends on flights from the United States, but deliveries average about four per week. Arrivals are heralded by a "happy face" sign and a "happy face" flag in front of the post office. If none is expected, the signboard carries a sad face. In John's words, "It's enough to make you throw up."

In a less cute manner, the radio and TV stations also announce

The recently remodeled telephone exchange

mail calls, which are held as soon as the mail is processed by the mail clerks. It is delivered not to residents but to "work centers," from where it is disseminated.

Since 1981, residents have been able to communicate directly with the outside world, thanks to a satellite communications system. Overseas phone calls can be made from home, office, or one of the twenty booths located on both sides of the bay. A three-minute conversation to the States costs from three to five dollars and is usually clearer than calling across the bay on "Gitmo Bell."

Military personnel can also make calls after working hours via the base's communications satellite facility. One such fifteen-minute "morale call" is permitted per week.

Free calls are possible, too. Residents can call 2176 and request that one of the radio "ham" operators line up a phone patch with a "ham" operator in the States. The only charge, if any, is between the Stateside resident and the Stateside radio operator.

There's also telegram service on the base and free teletype letter service that allows personnel to transmit as many as twenty-five words via MARS, the military affiliate radio system.

With such communication possibilities, Gitmo isn't as isolated as may first appear.

"So keep in touch," the captain reminded us new arrivals, suggesting he was weary of soothing the fears of worried relatives.

"Now, there's a subject I'd rather not have to mention," he continued ominously. "Most of the cases that come before me for nonjudicial punishment have to do with alcohol. So be forewarned. Enjoy your clubs, but don't overdo it." After a heavy, dramatic pause, he added drugs to his hit list. There wasn't a serious drug problem on the base, he assured us, although there were always "some bad apples in any barrel." Fifteen such tainted fruit were arrested at Gold Hill Barracks on October 25, 1972, for possession of marijuana. Five years later, marijuana-scenting dogs arrived.

"Your tour at Gitmo will be what you make it," he concluded, "And now you'll see a film history about Guantánamo Bay, prepared by our public affairs people." He stepped down from the dais and marched out looking as though relieved that his *Mission Impossible* was over.

The escorting petty officer shouted, "Attention on deck!"

Another attendant pulled a blackout curtain across the windows, creating a hothouse setting for the Navy's depiction of Gitmo's history.

Five

*W*HEN the film finished, the harsh fluorescent lights flickered on in the classroom and the new arrivals filed out, looking somewhat shell-shocked. Unsticking the shirt from my back, I followed along the corridor, lined by the DOD poster series I AM AN AMERICAN. One had the composite face of Lincoln and a determined fighter pilot. Below it, the copy read:

I AM AN AMERICAN,
DEFENDER OF FREEDOM

"Our defense is in the spirit which
prizes liberty as the heritage of all
men, in all lands everywhere."
—*Abraham Lincoln, 1858*

When I returned to the pickup, John was napping, his white hat pushed down over his eyes.

"Well," he asked as I opened the door, "did it leave a lump in your throat?"

I smiled and made no commitment.

"Our office produced that propaganda, you realize. Before my time, of course. I wouldn't have had anything to do with that."

As we started backing up, a gray pickup whipped in beside us.

"What are you doing parked here?" the young policeman shouted across the front seat of his truck.

"Just leaving," John waved, quickly reversing.

As we sped away, we could see the cop noting on his clipboard the serial number of our bumper sticker.

"Gestapo! He's writing out a report! The chief swore he'd send me to the boat shed if I got another one!"

Once John had calmed down, he admitted that the chief probably couldn't send anyone to the boat shed that was rumored to be manned by big, sadistic boatswain's mates. But the chief could have John's driver's license revoked for accumulating more than twelve driving points within a year.

"Why do they always have to catch *me?*"

When we arrived at the barracks, we found my two roommates still in the sack. In the bunk under mine, a dark-blond sailor sat cross-legged, seemingly in meditation.

"Who's that?" I mouthed like a character in a silent comedy.

John was not as considerate, commenting loudly, "He's a security pig, they say. But no one knows for sure. He doesn't speak to anyone. Everyone's a security risk."

"How's that?"

"He can't afford to make friends. They might try to take advantage of his position," John explained. "What puzzles me is why they put him in here with us. Maybe he's a spy sent by the chief." Countering my skepticism, he grinned. "You never know."

Despite our presence, the hairy Buddha remained undisturbed. Had he become deaf as well as silent in his meditation?

John walked over to the opposite bunk and shook it violently. A black fist swung at him from the white-sheet cocoon on the top. "This sack artist is our illustrious electronics technician. Some men drink; others prefer to retreat into sleep. Hey!" he shouted again at the bunk. "Wake up and meet your new boss."

A black head slowly lifted from under the sheet and turned toward us. Wearing a piece of nylon stocking stretched over his hair, the ET (electronics technician) blinked, frowned, and curled back into his shroud.

"He's even more charming when he's awake! But you better learn to coddle him if you want to keep the equipment up."

When I opened my locker door, John peered in. "You haven't got a Gitmo Gal calendar!" he said with alarm. "Hang tight. I'll be right back."

He darted out and returned carrying a mimeographed sheet of paper. "Here she is!"

I examined the figure of a woman divided into 365 tiny, puzzle-like sections for each day of the year.

"Thanks," I said, handing the sheet of paper back to him, "but I really don't need it."

"You have to have one."

"Why?"

"You need to keep track of how many days you've got until you become a short-timer."

"Counting the days will make it seem longer."

"You don't understand, spider toes. You won't fit in unless you can tell everyone how many days and a wake-up you have left on the Rock. It's the one thing we all have in common."

Despite my objections, he took the calendar and taped it on the inside of my locker door where a previous one had been torn down.

"There you go, sailor. Shout when you're ready for chow."

He left me puzzling his attitude. Did his sarcasm and flippancy cloak resentment of me?

While we waited in the line along the porch of the mess hall, I noticed various numbers tattooed on the white posts as if the supporting uprights were used for some kind of primitive counting system. I didn't need John to explain. By listening to the chat, I discovered what was being counted so zealously:

"Who's forty-two and a wake-up?"

"Bubble Butt, I think."

"I didn't know he was a short-timer!"

"Just imagine: forty-two days."

"Yeah. How long have you got?"

It was obvious what the unmarried men and those unaccompanied by their families thought about their Gitmo tour of duty.

Inside the dining facility, I found that even the food at Gitmo has unique aspects . . . and for good reason. Most food and all supplies must be shipped in from the States on a containerized cargo ship of the Seatrain Lines. Its arrival every two weeks is a big event in the life of the residents. The commissary store, if closed, opens its doors. Residents flock in like frontiersmen eager to restock.

Before the containerized ships began operating in 1972, delivery took from two to three weeks. Produce arrived spoiled, so the Navy tried flying in frozen goods, but this proved to be too expensive. With Seatrain, some perishables and frozen foods are carried in refrigerated vans, which reduces unloading time, pilferage, and damage from excessive handling.

On occasion, lettuce, ice cream, and other perishables arrived by Air Force C-141's and C-130's. Sometimes the VC-10 pilots manage to "smuggle" in the precious cargo when returning from missions abroad.

Quality milk products, like vegetables, have always been in short supply. From 1914 to 1944, the base had its own dairy. But when dependents were evacuated during World War II, the dairy was closed and powdered milk was substituted. After the war, the Exchange operated a powdered milk plant; however, base residents didn't go for the chalky white substance. Both frozen and concentrated milk were tried and met with a similar hostile reception. Next, fresh milk was imported, but this attempt also failed.

As a result, Gitmo was forced to put in a milk plant, which began operating in 1967. Called the "mechanical cow" by Cuban residents, the facility churns out regular and low fat milk, chocolate milk, yogurt, sour cream, and cottage cheese.

By a process termed "filled milk," milk powder and vegetable fat are combined to approximate a product comparable in texture and taste to whole milk. Once combined, the mixture is pasteurized, then forced through a homogenizer to keep the fat from separating. The taste takes "getting used to," as the Navy puts it.

Some 2600 gallons of such filled milk products are produced daily by the mechanical cow. Cheese, eggs, and ice cream have to be shipped in on Seatrain. Small wonder that the opening of a Baskin-Robbins ice cream parlor in one of the mini-mart stores became a major event of 1980.

The three mini-marts also sell fresh bread—100 to 130 loaves daily—which is baked on the base. (Gitmo had a full-fledged bakery between 1967 and 1972, but it was shut down because it was too expensive to operate.) Frozen breads and other bakery products are shipped in.

Both milk and vegetables are highly valued because they aren't readily available. Often those people who miss milk and vegetables the most are the ones who wouldn't touch the stuff under normal circumstances.

Because of the lack of fresh produce, some residents struggle to cultivate small vegetable gardens that can yield year round if the plants survive in the hot, dry climate. Gardening at Gitmo takes hard, dedicated work. The topsoil is only about a foot deep and the ground seems as impenetrable as the rest of Cuba.

Tropical fruits do grow on the base, including mangoes, avocados, papayas, bananas, oranges, grapefruit, guavas, pomegranates, and limes. Quantities, however, are so small that Gitmo could never be mistaken for a Garden of Eden.

Fish, on the other hand, is plentiful, and fishing provides welcomed recreation in addition to fresh food for the table. The great barracuda, tarpon, kingfish, jack, snook, and several kinds of snappers and groupers are the most common game fish. At least one world record fish has been taken from Guantánamo Bay, and a few

The barracuda is one of many varieties of game fish. It also represents a danger to anyone swimming outside the netted areas.

The Stoplight Inn is a fast food restaurant operated by the Navy Exchange.

big sailfish have been caught in nearby waters. Despite the availability, however, fresh fish are not sold on the base. You have to catch your own or settle for frozen.

Guantánamo Bay also offers a special challenge for fishermen: trapping langosta. These small, tasty lobsters of the Caribbean, a popular treat for the locals, can be taken from August 1 to February 28.

Despite having what less fortunate Caribbean people would consider an abundance, Gitmo residents aren't content. They miss junk food, especially the all-American hamburger as only a fast food franchise can serve it. Personnel returning from a trip to the States have been known to bring back coolers full of hamburgers which can be warmed up in a microwave or oven. The Navy Exchange coffee shop offers a two-patty hamburger called the Gitmo burger, and takeout pizza and grilled chicken are sold at various spots around the base, but they're not the same as real American junk, not the same as home.

To help compensate for such deprivations, a wealth of recreation is provided. Unfortunately, because of work loads and schedules, some have less opportunity than others to enjoy it.

After a swim in the barracks pool, John and I returned to the TV station where John continued my indoctrination. He warned me, among other things, not to expect much cooperation from the crew and to be prepared to sign on unassisted. I listened respectfully, but I thought he was probably exaggerating.

As the time neared, however, I found his assessment to be spot on. And I was relieved he was there to perform the daily ritual that I was yet to learn. Apparently my suspicions of concealed resentment were unfounded. He turned up the levels on the control panel, twisting the knobs and pushing buttons, as Guber watched surreptitiously from the adjoining studio.

The national anthem played and national monuments paraded across the monitor screen. Flipping a switch on the control panel, John leaned down to the microphone and announced, "This is the television station of the United States Armed Forces at Guantánamo Bay, beginning our broadcast day."

He pushed the switch back and said to me, "Do you think anybody would mistake it for anything else? NBC, maybe?"

While Captain Marvel battled the enemies of the nation, the crew traipsed through the side door into the projection room and began stowing food and cans of soda in their wall lockers.

"Hail, hail, the gang's all here!" John sang out.

They replied with a short burst of the unofficial Navy hymn.

Taking their time, they sauntered into the control room, giving me contemptuous looks as they took up their positions. They already knew of the chief's personnel change, thanks to Ski, who had broken the speed limit driving to the barracks to spread the word. Nevertheless, John made the official announcement, and the crew grumbled and cursed on cue.

"No tears," John protested. "In closing, let me say that I expect you all to give your new supervisor as much cooperation as you've given me."

They didn't share his sarcastic brand of humor.

While two of the crew positioned themselves on the stools at the control panel, the others moseyed into the studio and began setting up for the nightly news and *Command Quiz.*

"If this building wasn't air-conditioned, I wonder if they would report for duty at all," John said to me. "Well, we better go see what slides our anchor man is using tonight."

I followed, wondering if it was too late for me to volunteer for fence-line duty.

The news that evening began with what seemed to be a comedy of errors. The face of the newscaster, the JO in charge of the news department, popped up on the monitor; his lips moved in earnest, but he couldn't be heard. John, who was showing me how to direct the program, accused the crew of not properly testing the microphones.

"Next time, test 'em yourself."

"It could be a loose plug," John granted and hurried out of the control room into the studio.

He edged himself behind the backdrop, painted to give the impression that the news reader sat in front of an absurd window view of skyscrapers. The canvas rippled. Midway through a sentence, the reporter's words came into the control room.

The skyscrapers shook again, suggesting an earthquake had struck, as John found his way out from behind the backdrop.

"Now, live from San Francisco!" One of the crewmen laughed, sitting at the control board. When he punched up the next slide, it appeared upside down on the screen. He quickly tried to correct his mistake, but hit the polarization knob instead, switching the subject of the slide into negative.

In the studio, the newscaster looked up at the monitor, saw the foul up, and lost his place in the script.

John rushed back into the control room. "Go to the next slide!"

The previous transparency, however, popped up. The crewman tried to regain the proper sequence, but the slides were hopelessly out of order. The Secretary of State appeared when a South American dictator should have been the subject on the screen. Then the President smiled, instead of a long-haired leader of a religious cult in India.

Striving to disguise his anxiety, the news reader stumbled on until the end of his copy.

"And that's the shape of the world today," he concluded, looking very much relieved.

73

As the music and credits rolled, he cursed the crew and left scowling.

Simultaneously, Don Alfredo danced in, wearing Bermuda shorts and, for the benefit of the cameras, a sports coat and tie. His varying sets of clothes produced the effect of an amalgamation of two different bodies, much like the figures on the DOD posters.

After a couple of adroit cha-cha-cha's, he flopped into the news reader's chair. He positioned his news copy on the desk in front of him and clowned at the cameras during the playing of the taped introduction for *Noticias en Español*.

He began, projecting a radiant face, serious but upbeat. He spat out the words with expertise and flare. Professionalism seemed restored until a pair of hands reached out from under the backdrop and started pulling the white hair that resembled shredded coconut sprinkled on his tanned legs. He looked as if he had switched from the cha-cha to the mambo as he tried to kick his tormentors without losing his smile. His inflections hit new heights.

In the control room, the crew laughed and applauded.

"What's going on?" John shouted into his headset.

One of the cameramen pointed to the hands under the table.

John was exasperated. "Now you see what you'll have to deal with," he told me. He started for the door, but the telephone stopped him.

"That'll be the chief."

He picked up the receiver. "Control room. Yes, Chief. Oh, just some technical problems."

All of us could hear the chief shouting at the other end of the line.

"Yes, Chief. Yes, Chief . . ."

When John hung up, he told the giggling crew, "I hope you bird droppings are satisfied."

"This is almost as good as the time the curtains caught on fire during *Cooking with the Commander*," one of the crew said. "First time the fire department had ever been on TV!"

John chewed on his disgust. "You know, I'm going to miss this job like another year on the Rock."

The telephone started ringing again, and Don Alfredo danced on

Testing a microphone for the
Christmas TV Special

through the news until John went out and grabbed the culprits—a
scene the cameramen made sure the audience didn't miss.

Once the first filmed program started, John suggested we get
something to eat from the Morin Center takeout next door, since
we had missed dinner. As we left, my roommate, the ET, arrived
with a giant pizza combination and a family-sized paper cup of beer.
His was flagrant defiance of the chief's decree that there was to be
no eating in the control room. Someone had spilled a cola drink on
the panel, gumming up the instruments, John told me, adding,
"Just imagine what that stuff does to your insides. I wonder if they've
ever considered using it in chemical warfare?"

Next door, the open air dining area was quickly filling up with
fleet sailors and Marines. Sitting at the tables with their beer,
sandwiches, pizza, and fried chicken, they waited boisterously for
the first show of the evening to begin on the outdoor stage.

"They ought to call this the Moron Center," John observed.

The center once had offered a chance for residents and visitors
to dine, by reservation, indoors, at a supper club where they could
enjoy a surprising choice of food and wine, often augmented by a
cabaret act. Today, Gitmo's "formal" eating establishment is the
Blue Caribe family restaurant next to the runway on McCalla Road.
It features a menu of steaks, seafood, and other entrees with a salad
bar. Also at the Blue Caribe is the Patio Lounge, with disco entertainment on weekends.

Somewhat down the scale of Gitmo elegance is the Stoplight
Inn, located near the stoplight, which offers pizzas, fried chicken,
short orders, and steam table entrees in a cafeteria setting. There

A recent menu for the Blue Caribe family restaurant

is also a takeout window. Next to the hangar at Leeward Point is a similar eating place, called the Kountry Kitchen. The Staff Noncommissioned Officers' Club also has a takeout window for fast food, which is available to all base residents. In addition to the coffee shop, already mentioned, there are a number of snack shacks throughout the base, including those at the hospital, bowling alley, golf course, and enlisted swimming pool. As this suggests, eating is one of the favorite pastimes in the languorous environment.

After joining the mob at what rivaled a German beer garden, John and I stayed for the first performance of the floor show: Spanish flamenco dancers and a singer who had made a successful recording of "Spanish Eyes."

The audience responded enthusiastically to the troupe's performance, although many had seen it several times before. By the end of my Gitmo tour, I felt as though I could perform the dance numbers and sing "Spanish Eyes" in my sleep. Coincidentally, I encountered the singer at a cocktail party in Spain some years later. He insisted he had enjoyed his Gitmo experience, implying that it had nothing to do with his decision to give up singing and become a painter. And I assured him my Gitmo experience was not the reason for my failure to pursue a career in television or journalism.

Six

*A*S well as an illicit fast-food franchise, the TV studio often became Gitmo's unofficial movie preview theatre after the evening's live programming. In an uncharacteristic burst of energy, the crew set up folding chairs, screen, and projector and assembled with their forbidden food and beer.

The admiral's driver delivered the film, which he had obtained from his contact in the film library before any segments deemed too stimulating could be censored. According to the scuttlebutt, the admiral's wife served as the chief censor, and the crew liked to picture her and her cronies, scissors at the ready, scrutinizing the films at afternoon tea parties.

Through the admiral's driver we were also treated to privileged information, especially gossip and important command decisions before they were officially announced, such as a special DEFEX held to demonstrate Gitmo's preparedness to a visiting group of United States Congressmen.

"O-five-hundred hours," the driver insisted was the time, assuring the skeptics in the group that he had heard it straight from the Old Man's mouth.

On the night before the mobilization, the crew debated whether to camp out at the station overnight or return to the barracks, which would mean a hassle getting back in the morning when Sherman Avenue would be choked with cars as men rushed to their duty stations.

Those of us who opted for a few hours in the sack left after sign-off, while the others, supplied with enough junk food and drink to wait out several mobilizations, remained behind playing cards and darts and reminiscing over DEFEX's past.

Long before the sirens sounded, the barracks lights came on. Pops and his strikers trooped down the corridors bellowing for everyone to roll out. I swung down from my bunk, being careful not to shake up Buddha below, but he apparently had already dressed and gone. Sometimes I thought I was living with an apparition, particularly when I said hello to him in the mornings and got no response. Since I was supposed to be a specialist in communications, I felt like a failure and questioned if I had missed out on something by not receiving my training at the DOD information school.

As I joined the procession of the living dead toward the showers, a bewildered new arrival pleaded, "What's the lights on for? What's going on?"

"The Old Man's invited us all to breakfast," retorted one of the zombies shuffling past.

"Your first DEFEX, huh?" another mused.

"What's that?" the uninitiated wanted to know, but no one could be bothered to enlighten him at that time of the morning.

Someone coming in from late night duty shouted that the mess hall was open. And as if cued, the smell of fresh bread and cinnamon rolls wafted through the barracks.

I hurried to join those who felt like eating.

Back at the barracks, Pops, red faced with exasperation and a hangover, admonished his brood of sleepy sailors. Two of the nervous new members of November Company, part of the frontline provisional defense forces, grabbed their oversized helmets off the top of their lockers. Fumbling to adjust the slings of their rifles, they rushed down the corridor through a gauntlet of jibes. Their

78

Marines of the Ground Defense Force mobilize along the fence line.

camouflage fatigues, much too big for them, reminded me of hand-me-downs from older brothers.

"Who dressed ya?" someone shouted at them.

"I'm glad you guys are on our side!"

November Company and its sister company Quebec are rifle companies of Navy men who serve in customary duty assignments on the base. During DEFEX drills and in the event of attack, the members of these companies are called up, something like the reserves, to augment the ground defense forces.

Outside the barracks, the "reservists" joined the company of sailors, visually if not actually transformed into combat soldiers, who had formed up in the road. The men smoked and attempted jokes as they waited impatiently to reinforce their traditional enemies, the Marines, on the fence line and at fortified positions throughout the hills.

Personnel carriers, like over-fed maternal insects, maneuvered into position to load them.

Suddenly, the DEFEX siren screamed, chilling the muggy morning with a blast like an air raid warning.

Led by fearless John, the AFRTS/*Gazette* staffs piled into the station's pickup and van, and we fought our way onto Sherman

Avenue. John blew the horn and cursed as he tried to part the traffic that looked like a string of bug eyes streaming toward the mother nest. "What a joke," a voice beside me complained in the morning gloom. "One direct hit on this highway and the Cubans could paralyze the entire base."

"Don't sweat it. Castro doesn't want this hole."

"What makes you think so?"

"He couldn't afford the prices in the commissary."

When we eventually arrived at the station, we found those who had spent the night there looking as if they had already been through the DEFEX. But their alertness didn't matter much since we had little to do except don our combat helmets and wait—as is the case in any respectable military exercise.

Our job at AFRTS during the defensive exercise was to provide music and to relay through news bulletins any instructions to base residents. From us they would learn whether they could resume their daily routine or start evacuating. In the meantime, we all waited.

With their helmets tipped down over their eyes, the TV crew dozed at the control panel while slides depicted familiar scenes of the United States—Mount Rushmore, Valley Forge, the Washington Monument, and the like—with patriotic and popular music patched in from Guber's turntable next door. I could only guess at who had chosen this programming and why. Was it designed to inspire the troops? Demoralize the enemy? As far as I could see, all it accomplished was to put people to sleep. But, as an old military maxim goes, one's job is not to reason why . . .

After several monotonous hours, some of the crew got one of their rare ambitious ideas. We could improve our DEFEX coverage by taking the cameras outside and capturing some of the action for the folks waiting anxiously at home. I was dubious but insecure enough in my unwanted position to cave in to popular demand.

We opened the side doors to the studio and rolled the two cameras into the gathering heat as far as their umbilical cords would permit. (The station didn't have remote capability at that time.) We managed to pick up the movement of military vehicles on

Sherman Avenue and the dust from tanks churning across the hills. Someone suggested we call the VC-10 squadron and ask the pilots to make a flyover for the program, but I had enough sense to squelch that idea.

I was soon called into the studio: "You're wanted on the horn!"

John stood by smirking as I took the call from the chief, who had finagled his way into the group of VIP's observing the exercise from the situation room of the command center. Unfortunately for him, he got more action than he'd bargained for. Someone telephoned the admiral to question our broadcast. (The crew accused the Gitmo film board.) The Old Man, in turn, demanded to know what we were doing. Was it too difficult for the Cubans to watch us from their observation posts? Did we have to make it easier for them by putting it all on television? Was the mobilization merely another dreadful AFRTS program?

I felt sympathy for the chief and apologized for my lack of judgment. But he dismissed my explanation and ordered us all to be on hand after the DEFEX.

When he handed out the punishment later, he put us on working parties to paint and spruce up the station and vowed to reject any request for R & R (Rest and Recreation).

"So, what's new?" one of the incorrigibles commented, risking a trip to the boat shed. The chief had forgotten that every recent request for R & R had been turned down because the crew was deemed indispensable to the AFRTS operation.

My punishment was for me to continue on as before: working twelve hours or more a day with a crew as cooperative as that of the H.M.S. *Bounty.*

It took years for anyone to appreciate our efforts to cover the Gitmo defensive forces in action. But in 1981 we were vindicated when both sides of the fence vied for media coverage during a Caribbean military exercise involving the United States, Britain, France, and five Latin American countries. When the Cuban Government learned that the United States had banned reporters from the operations, Castro quickly invited the reporters to cover the Gitmo part of the maneuvers from the Cuban side of the fence.

Marines in training prepare to come ashore by helicopter.

The United States countered by opening Gitmo to reporters.

Not since the Cuban Missile Crisis had Gitmo received so much attention. TV crews talked to one another with two-way radios across the Cactus Curtain. Base residents enjoyed the rare chance of watching themselves on national television, broadcast via satellite from the Cuban side of the fence to the United States and back to Gitmo. The Cubans weren't so lucky. They had to watch themselves on Channel 8—our AFRTS. Such are the deprivations of Cuban socialism, as John would have said.

It's not often that a military exercise pushes Gitmo center stage, but it does happen, as the 1981 maneuvers indicate. Another instance occurred in 1979 when President Carter ordered in the 38th Marine Amphibious Unit after it became known that a Soviet brigade was stationed in Cuba. Some 1500 Marines came ashore at

Gitmo by helicopter, while another 250 landed in amphibious tractors.

Happily for residents, the Marines were more accurate in their work than the accompanying task force of sixty journalists. A reporter from Massachusetts wrote that "The base was constructed in 1962, after the Cuban Missile Crisis, and most of it looks like it hasn't been used since. Except for a modern elementary school, many of the buildings look ramshackle and in need of repair."

Even the representative from the prestigious *Washington Post* couldn't get the facts straight, writing: "The base was built after the Cuban Missile Crisis, and it looks like it hasn't been used since. Grass is growing through the floors of buildings, ripped screens flap in the breeze and suggestions with what to do with the place are painted on the sides of buildings."

Small wonder the press doesn't get invited more often.

Because of all the publicity, concerned relatives telephoned from the States to ask if everything was all right and wanting to know what was going to happen. One Naval officer was quoted as answering, "We are just about to go swimming." Another serviceman said all he intended to do was to keep his teenaged daughter indoors while the Marines were about. Some people tended to forget the Marines were on *our* side.

The uproar over the Soviet troops soon subsided into a whimper. The United States did nothing further about the situation, and, after it was over, the base commander admitted knowing about the brigade eights months prior to the official announcement in Washington. He felt the Soviet presence was no cause for alarm. Many members of Congress agreed, adding that the U.S. show of force had been a waste of the taxpayer's money.

But this opinion hasn't stopped the government from ordering similar military maneuvers, including Ocean Venture, part of the series of war games held during 1983–84 to "demonstrate and improve the capability of the United States to protect and maintain the free use of the sea lines of communication in the Caribbean Basin and the Gulf of Mexico."

Ocean Venture, which cost some $25 million, included a Marine

The 38th Marine Amphibious Unit hits the beach at Gitmo during the reinforcement exercise of October, 1979.

reinforcement of Gitmo and the evacuation of three hundred women and children to Jacksonville, Florida. They spent three days there before returning from a kind of a windfall R & R.

As well as acts of man, acts of nature may create the need for a DEFEX, although in the latter case residents only have to vacate their homes for a nearby shelter. But they still must sweat out the nerve-racking hours waiting until it can be pinpointed where the storm will strike. The suspense and anxiety mount as the commanding officer announces increasing degrees of alert preparedness. If he is forced to set Condition One, all those in unprotected housing must move in with friends who live in hurricane-proof quarters, or go to one of the thirty-five hurricane shelters.

The CO also orders all ships in port to anchor in the bay away from piers and wharves. (Since it was discovered, the harbor has protected ships seeking refuge from the frequent hurricanes in the Caribbean.)

Then, it's the CO's turn to move. He takes his operational command post to a bombproof shelter where he and his staff can direct disaster control operations.

Similarly, the commanding officer of the Marines and his staff set up a command post underground to direct the security of the base. Among other things, the commandant directs the guards on the fence line to take up positions in special storm bunkers.

In its underground hospital, the base medical staff receives pregnant women and infants. The Public Works Department readies its repair crews. The Fire Department stands by for emergencies, usually fires from downed power lines.

The base police ensure that all residents have left nonhurricane-proof housing. Invariably, they have to deal with oddball calls, too, such as the one from a woman who asked for a policeman to come and roll up car windows because she didn't want to go outside and get wet during the storm.

Gitmo's most devastating hurricane was Inez, which struck the base on September 30, 1966. Roofs buckled while trees and power lines snapped in the 100-knot wind gusts. Eight inches of torrential rain fell in ten hours. Although Leeward Point was within two miles of the eye of the storm, there were no injuries. Nearby islands weren't so lucky. A thousand people were killed and thousands left homeless in Haiti and the Dominican Republic.

But most of the time, Gitmo's tempests are those in teapots, which visiting politicians and reporters are likely to discover if they're paying attention. One wonders, at times, such as during the first DEFEX to be carried "live" on TV, when I was selected to have lunch with my congressman. (He wasn't actually from my district back home but he was from the state, which apparently was the best the Navy could do under the circumstances.)

On the appointed day I donned pristine tropical dress whites and walked to the mess hall for what was billed as a typical meal.

The galley MAA, also uncomfortable in his white uniform, stood watch at the door. I had never seen him out of dungarees. Glowering as though I was one of those responsible, he directed me to an area cordoned off for the special guests.

Behind the steam tables on the serving line, the cooks and the assistant potato peelers stood smartly at parade rest. Wearing cook's hats and starched white aprons, they had never looked so clean and neat. Only the sweat trickling down their greasy faces appeared as usual.

I noticed, too, that the aluminum and chrome shone with the

evidence of extra cleaning. The linoleum had been waxed and buffed beyond the exacting demands of the Navy to the standard of TV commercials for floor polish. New red-and-white checkered table-cloths dressed the tables John liked to call feeding troughs.

Next to a vase of tiny wild flowers, I found a place card with the name of my state and sat down, feeling creases decimating my perfect whites.

A young sailor soon joined me. After revealing our hometowns and length of time spent at Gitmo, we sat silently waiting as the mess hall officially opened and our shipmates streamed in, gawking at us and the tarted-up surroundings.

When the congressional party arrived, the admiral and his staff led them to the head of the serving line. Laughing and enjoying themselves, the congressmen and the reporters accompanying them looked like American tourists in the tropics. They had on breezy short-sleeve shirts with big gaudy patterns and Bermuda shorts to match.

Suddenly the admiral's aide broke away from the beaming party and rushed over to our table. "Your congressman has been detained on the golf course," he whispered so no one nearby could hear. Then he asked us to get up and leave quietly so it wouldn't be too obvious what had happened. We did, feeling relieved from a torture. It wasn't until later, while devouring a Gitmo burger at the coffee shop, that I thought about the shabby treatment and billing Congress for the cost of my lunch.

John loved the episode and danced around the newsroom when I told him, giggling like Ski. But he got his, as we used to say, that evening when one of the reporters paid us a visit.

After the obligatory tour of the facility, John cornered the reporter in the newsroom and attempted to fill his ears with Gitmo gossip, injustice, scandal, and corruption. There were lots of juicy tidbits John could supply that weren't in the official press kit. The reporter, however, wasn't interested.

"Can you tell me what time the duty free shop closes?" he asked to John's chagrin. "I haven't had time to get any cigarettes and liquor."

Seven

LIKE many servicemen during their Gitmo tour, I spent most of my time working or sleeping, as already indicated. My enjoyment of the "amusement park" was limited to an occasional movie or visit to the beach. Weeks passed and I saw little except the AFRTS station and the barracks, and Sherman Avenue in between. Most of the other unmarried journalists on the staff would say the same, although the lack of variety in their lives was due to their preference for spending off-duty hours drinking beer or sleeping. But it's easy to become lethargic in a place like Gitmo, where the climate and daily routine always seem to be the same.

One afternoon, however, John decided it was time I had the five-dollar base tour. We drove in the AFRTS pickup, which by this point was like a moving target for the base police, along Sherman Avenue, past "Sears," to Bulkeley Hill. Because the perimeter is off limits, we took our 35-mm cameras to help create the pretext of being journalists on assignment.

The Northeast Gate, I discovered when we crested Bulkeley Hill, lies in a kind of campo, hidden from the rest of the base. The area is desolate and sparse, with dry grass, cactus, scrub, and few trees other than the small varieties on the nearby hills. Accompanied by a dirt road, the fence line snakes across this campo-like area, climbing east to the coastal hills. To the west, it disappears over hills

The Water Gate, the only gap in the fence line, permits merchant ships to reach the upper part of Guantánamo Bay and the port city of Caimanera.

and after a brief pause at the bay continues on the Leeward side and ends on the high coastal cliffs above the Windward Passage.

Watchtowers, spaced far apart, and other sentry posts face one another across this demarcation of galvanized wire, conjuring up long-legged invaders from H. G. Wells's *War of the Worlds*. One Marine, carrying the typical field equipment and M-16 rifle, mans each of the forty-five posts, in addition to those who patrol on foot and in jeeps. Waiting to report any Cuban activity is boring but crucial to the security of the base. At night, sentry duty can be more exciting. There is no light, except for the moon, which is not welcomed because it distorts shadows. Nocturnal animals, particularly land crabs and snakes, cause jittery nerves. Sometimes horses and cows wander onto a post and get shot for failing to answer the sentry's challenge.

There are only two breaks in the ten-foot chain link barrier: the Northeast Gate and the "Water Gate," which refers not to dirty tricks but to a short gap created by two narrow channels on either side of Flamingo Cay leading to the upper part of the bay.

The Seabees built the present fence in 1953 as part of the treaty agreement that makes it the responsibility of the United States to maintain the boundary fences. Over the years some of the so-called "inner boundary" fences had been allowed to disintegrate. Cattle, horses, and goats roamed at will in the northern areas, and such wide-open spaces encouraged smuggling—a problem no longer.

A company of seventy to one hundred Marine guards, taken from the Marine Barracks total of four hundred, guards each of the Leeward and Windward sectors of the fence line. During their week of sentry duty, the men live near the fence line in a special barracks from which they are driven to their posts. Each man stands a four-to-six hour watch, periodically peering with high-powered binoculars at the Cuban side. (Equipment employed at night is classified, but undoubtedly the special hardware includes infra-red or light-enhancement devices.) Guard dogs, although used in the past, are no longer seen along the fence.

Beyond this boundary of the base, four fences in the Cuban sector of the frontier constitute the Cactus Curtain. Heading in the direction of Cuba, there are three fences, a barrier road, and another fence.

The Northeast Gate area, with the Marine Ground Defense Force barracks in the foreground. The "Cattle Chute," the path Cuban dayworkers must follow, is partially visible between the checkpoint, center, and the cleared patch of the hill, upper left, behind which is the Cuban processing facility.

Lomo Pictoe, a 500-foot hill to the east of the base, enables Cuban soldiers to view more than 80 percent of Gitmo.

Since 1964, when they pulled back from the Northeast Gate, the Cubans have added concentric circles of minefields, observation towers, and surveillance positions carved into the bases of hillsides with tunnels for exit and entry. They also have built artillery lairs, underground concrete revetments to accommodate Soviet SU-100 self-propelled artillery, in the hills paralleling the fence line. It is not known, however, if guns have ever been installed.

Cuban officials say small army units operate in this Cuban zone of hundreds of cleared acres. Their primary mission it to observe and record the movements of U.S. military personnel and equipment on and off the base. Visiting American journalists have reported that Cuban guards apparently are not equipped for their vigil with any devices other than high-powered binoculars and cameras. Most don't carry pistols or rifles, but bayonets and gas masks in canvas pouches dangle from their belts.

Leaving our hilltop panorama, we dropped down into the dreadful valley, crossing the minefield, its coils of barbed wire, red warning signs, and death concealed by the underbrush.

"Now crossing the world's largest minefield," John sang out

breezily, failing, however, to disguise that we were both awed and horrified. The twenty men who have died there since the mines were laid include Marines, sailors, and Cubans fleeing from repression.

The most tragic case happened during the Water Crisis of 1964. Five sailors from the U.S.S. *Boxer* became disoriented while walking back to the ship from a beach outing early in the evening of May 2. Being unfamiliar with the restricted parts of the base, they wandered into the minefield. Marine sentries near the area heard the explosion and the screams of the victims. A second explosion was heard soon after the first. A helicopter with searchlights was dispatched to the area immediately but no survivors could be seen. The next day, a team of Marine demolition experts worked eight hours to clear a path through the minefield to the spot of the explosion and recovered the bodies.

Marines normally assigned to engineering duty are given the job of maintaining the deadly obstruction. Working methodically every day, these men check each mine and replace it if necessary. In this manner the Marine Corps estimates that every mine in the Gitmo field will be checked once every four years.

The Gitmo minefield, largest active minefield in the world, provides part of the base's fixed defenses.

As we approached the Northeast Gate, I was surprised to find it as quiet and sleepy as a general store along an interstate highway. I suppose I expected something like Checkpoint Charlie between East and West Berlin, but at that time of day the militarily tidy area appeared abandoned, despite the presence of a Marine barracks only a hundred yards distant where the Windward sentries live for the week they're on duty. Although there was no one in sight to challenge us, we knew we were being carefully scrutinized from both sides.

We parked near the bus-stop shelter and got out, brandishing our cameras. We walked to the end of Sherman Avenue, which loops around something like a golfing green with a telephone in place of a flag stuck in the middle. At the top of this loop, two sets of big wire gates secure the entry point. The Stars and Stripes on a tall flagpole unfurls above a sign declaring:

NORTH EAST GATE

MARINE BARRACKS

&

GROUND DEFENSE FORCE

U.S. NAVAL BASE

GUANTÁNAMO BAY, CUBA

"And I thought this was Kansas," John quipped.

A few yards behind the gate sits the abandoned Cuban building originally built in 1960 as a bank for Cuban commuters to exchange their American dollars into pesos. Its rippled concrete roof, like a piece of oversized corrugated cardboard bleached white in the sun, protrudes on either side of a square arch bearing the tidings:

REPUBLICA DE CUBA

TERRITORIA LIBRE DE AMERICA

The Cuban workers were searched in this building after the closing of the frontier in 1959. During these inspections, workers who were smuggling contraband (usually Band-Aids and aspirin for their families) would pitch the items over the fence to avoid getting caught. This and most aspects of the search procedure could be observed

The Northeast Gate, with Marine sentry box, and the former Cuban processing facility

easily by reporters from the American side and were often photographed.

With the formal break in relations between the two countries in 1961, fence-line security changed, although at first it was less severe than it became later. In the beginning, the Cuban Government placed young, inexperienced militia along the perimeter. Poorly clothed and ill-equipped, the men often chatted with the Marines and accepted cigarettes through the links in the fence.

But, in September of 1962, the Cubans got tougher. They pulled back their inspection operation to a series of barracks-like structures hidden behind a hill about a mile from the gate. And they built a concrete path, lined by a chain link fence, called the Cattle Chute, along which the commuters were forced to walk from the inspection buildings to the gate. At the same time, the Cuban Government stopped the small ferry boats that had been bringing workers from Caimanera and Boquerón to the main pier at Gitmo. A campaign of harassment had begun.

As already mentioned, Cuban workers had to rise early in the morning to catch buses to take them from their villages and towns to the hidden changing shed. They were forced to strip before Cuban inspectors, then walk naked along an L-shaped corridor to a changing room where they were given "Navy base" clothes. No personal effects were allowed, not even glasses, which also had to be changed for a second pair to wear on the base.

The strip searches particularly intimidated and angered the women, forcing them eventually to quit their jobs. One of the last to leave was an office worker who had held her Gitmo job since 1942.

Recently, the strip searches have stopped, according to one of the remaining eighty-eight commuters. The examinations are now more like a spot-check, akin to going through United States customs.

But the commuters still have to walk down the Cattle Chute, crossing no-man's-land where Brahman cattle roam freely, to reach the Northeast Gate. The grade is so steep that homeward bound workers must stop and rest.

It's a tough way to earn a buck, particularly since the commuters must convert their Gitmo wages into virtually worthless pesos at a one-to-one exchange rate, resulting in a 90 percent loss of buying power. Time-consuming medical exams and inoculations have also been used as harassment.

Why, one wonders, do they persist? The answer is for a job, a well-paid job, including such benefits as shopping privileges in the Navy Exchange and the commissary—privileges that some Gitmo residents don't always appreciate, such as when there's no tuna fish or peanut butter. The area from which Cubans come, on the other hand, is impoverished, with food shortages and little hope for employment. While at Gitmo, the Cuban men can stuff themselves on gringo grub, eating enough to last them twenty-four hours so their families can have their meager food ration.

Another plus for keeping the job is that the commuters can use the post office to communicate with relatives and friends who have fled to other countries, primarily the United States.

How the Navy benefits from the commuters is easy to understand: it gets dependable skilled labor at a low price. Understanding why the Cuban Government allows the situation to continue, however, is more difficult to fathom. The usual explanation is the lack of work in Cuba and the need for American dollars. But are such few jobs and so little money worth the Cuban Government's trouble? And if they are, why doesn't Castro issue additional work permits? Could Castro have spies planted among the commuters? Or could some workers be used by the United States to smuggle out information about Cuba? The possibilities encourage intriguing speculation.

When Castro gained power in 1959, about three thousand commuters were employed on the base in various maintenance, repair, and service jobs. Many were skilled technicians, welders, and electricians working on United States warships. During the revolution and the transition period, most remained dedicated to their jobs. Once absenteeism nearly caused a complete work stoppage on the base. This, in the last year of the Batista regime, was due to a general strike throughout the eastern end of Cuba that stopped all transportation. There was also a rise in sick leave during that pe-

Foundry worker Eligo Mafos, who has commuted to his Gitmo job since 1953, keeps an eye on the furnace.

riod, and some isolated incidents occurred. Employees were caught attempting to smuggle payroll data from the supply depot. One worker was fired for using anti-American slogans.

After the United States cut diplomatic relations, it will be recalled, Castro stopped the hiring of base commuters by refusing to issue any further work permits. As the commuters retired, they were not replaced, and attrition has slowly reduced the number. Upon reaching retirement age, some choose to remain on the base, as did a large number during the Missile Crisis. (Commuters are no longer allowed to retire at Gitmo.)

To replace the day workers, the Navy first tried to recruit Cuban exiles from San Juan, Puerto Rico. But the attempt was completely unsuccessful. So the Navy turned to Jamaica, although the training of the unskilled laborers willing to come to Gitmo has been a long and slow process. In 1984 there were 777 Jamaican workers living on the base and 17 of their dependents.

The 188 Cuban exiles who live on the base (about half are the wives and children of exiles) reside in their own little community. They are represented by a Cuban community board designed to ensure that their welfare is not forgotten by the Navy. Also, in an observance to mark the long-standing friendship between the Cuban workers and the American community on the base, Gitmo holds a Cuban-American Friendship Day each year on the Friday in January closest to January 28, the birthday of Cuba's national hero, José Martí. (Of course, Jamaican workers are not left out. Gitmo honors Jamaican Independence Day on the first Monday in August.)

The exiles seem not to be a sensitive issue for the Cuban Government. As evidence, the Navy cites the fact that in recent years many Cuban exiles living on the base visited their homeland (via another country) and returned to Gitmo without encountering any difficulties while in Cuba.

Unless the exiles are "productive members of the base," which means they must have a job, they are "required to depart to the place of their choice. They are under no pressure to leave, otherwise," which sounds a bit like *Catch-22*. Fortunately, some exceptions are made for humanitarian reasons.

The Cuban community may at times include defectors from home, although they aren't allowed to stay for long. Those granted political asylum are shipped out to the States.

Officially, the United States "neither confirms nor denies" the existence of any defectors on the base. To do so would be admitting to a violation of the treaty obligation to return Cuban fugitives. Such an admission of defectors would give the Cuban president a propaganda platform on which to harangue the United States for harboring "criminals" on the base and another reason to call for the return of Gitmo to Cuba. (In the early 1970's, however, the State Department estimated that fifty to sixty Cubans had used Gitmo to escape from Cuba.)

How the defectors reach the base is not officially revealed, for obvious reasons. But it's also obvious that they come over the fence or down the bay through the Water Gate, as demonstrated by those who have made it and those who have not.

Dressed in ethnic costume, the daughter of a Gitmo serviceman joins in Cuban-American Friendship Day activities.

Author visits the hole where the base water pipes were severed during the 1964 Water Crisis.

Published stories of defectors support this conjecture. In one such defection, a student from the University of Havana stole a semi-trailer bearing the sign TRANSPORTES NATIONALES (Government Transport) and drove it south from Havana, making stops to pick up other defectors. Cuban police supposedly didn't stop the truck because it was traveling during the religious holiday of the Three Kings.

Shooting started near Caimanera. One bullet went through the cab and killed one of the two drivers. The truck rolled to a stop and the freedom riders ran for the fence. Some said they began jumping out of the truck near the Caimanera cemetery; others said they waited until the truck got to the beach, about five miles south of the town. From there they walked and swam until they reached the base.

But some didn't make it. Cuban machine-gun fire killed three men and guard dogs tore apart one woman. About thirty people were captured. Seven of those who reached the base had to be hospitalized, which must have made it difficult for anyone (except possibly the former military government of Argentina) to deny their existence.

Another case tells of three boys about sixteen years of age who swam across the upper portion of the bay late one evening. Two of the boys didn't reach the guard post at the Water Gate. The Marines, however, pulled the survivor from the water. He remained at Gitmo and attended school, graduating in 1964, when he was given a scholarship from the Guantánamo Bay Scholarship Fund. He later entered the United States under sponsorship of a Naval officer and attended college in the Chicago area.

Another defector, a sailor, escaped by jumping from a Cuban freighter in the harbor at Barcelona, Spain. He sailed on numerous merchant ships until one day, to his chagrin, he found himself on a ship headed back for Cuba. He kept calm until the ship entered Guantánamo Bay, when he leaped over the side and was picked up by a Navy police boat. He obtained asylum and a free plane ride to the United States.

Such stories encourage more respect in tourists, such as John and me and those who come every Saturday to take photos on the fence line, although the barricade appears no more daunting physically than the typical security fence with three strands of barbed wire on top.

After taking turns posing for our "hero" pictures beside the fence, John ushered me to a hole in the ground buttressed with boards and cordoned off by loops of white-painted chain. A large sign beside the monument commemorated Admiral Bulkeley's response to Castro's attempted blackmail:

U.S. ANSWER TO CASTRO: GITMO WATER
LIBERATED FROM CUBA AT THIS POINT.
NAVY SECURED WATER 6 FEB 1964. PIPE
LINE CUT 18 FEB 1964.

As if to underscore the seriousness of those events, a heavily sandbagged defensive position is situated immediately behind the famous hole in the ground.

John insisted he take my photo in front of the hole. "Come on, smile. Just pretend you're standing next to the chief's head."

Eight

*A*FTER my visit to the fence line, John took me to check out Gitmo's night life. We joined the exodus from the barracks to the Downtown movie lyceum, one of four such open air theatres where films are shown nightly free of charge.

The giant screen loomed like the shadow of a dark sail over the commissary and Navy Exchange as the herd approached. A caressing breeze relieved the warm night, fulfilling the promise of tropical paradise. I took a deep breath . . . and inhaled the familiar smells of fresh popcorn and butter. At least this was one aspect of home we expatriates wouldn't be deprived of.

Armed with popcorn, beer, or soda, the barracks group quickly filled the canvas chairs in the orchestra section reserved for unaccompanied enlisteds. Other areas were cordoned off for families, chief petty officers, officers, and civilians except Jamaican workers who were relegated to the bleachers in the rear. Instead of apartheid, this arrangement was intended to provide seating for all groups in the Gitmo pecking order.

In addition to the outdoor theatres, four of the military clubs show films nightly for members and their guests. Civilian entertainers, sponsored by the Department of Defense, frequently visit the base and perform at the lyceums before the movie.

Gitmo has its live theatre, too. Although no one knows exactly

Gitmo's Little Theatre troupe

when the first amateur production was presented, members of the Guantánamo Bay Little Theater Company believe it has one of the longest, most productive careers of any amateur group in the Armed Forces. Records establish that the company was active in 1948, when it produced *Arsenic and Old Lace*. Recently, the group has gone on the road, traveling the coconut circuit to Haiti and Jamaica as part of a little theatre exchange program.

What to do after the movie or theatre? Visit your club, of course. All groups have their special clubs where members can dine and socialize at bargain prices.

The official enlisted club burned down in 1969. It was replaced

Como Club, for those with officer status, is located on Deer Point.

The Gitmo library

in 1972 by the Windjammer, a $2.5-million building reported to be the largest single structure built by the Seabees. To help celebrate its opening, four *Playboy* bunnies and a country and western band were flown in from Miami. The club has bars, a cocktail lounge, a restaurant, and family bingo once a week.

Another popular evening haunt is Marblehead Hall, Gitmo's 28-lane bowling alley. Both league and individual bowling are as big on the base as in any small American town.

The more studiously inclined can visit the base library, which is small but, like all libraries, offers a refuge for meditation. In search of such a haven, I peeked in one night and found my silent roommate there reading a famous novel about the sufferings of a German youth. Afraid he might think I was spying on him, I hid among the stacks until it was safe to leave undetected.

For those who want to further their education during their tour, off-duty education and training programs are available. These include evening classes through the Los Angeles Metropolitan College Overseas, which enables personnel to complete a certificate or Associate degree during their Gitmo stay. "Short courses" for college credit are also offered by the Old Dominion University of Norfolk, Virginia, and video telecourses in systems and organization management are provided by the Hampton Institute of Hampton, Virginia.

Despite such educational offerings, however, no one would ever mistake Gitmo for a college campus, even one of the "sun and fun" institutes popular in California or Florida. Most residents prefer to join one or more of the sixty special interest clubs and organizations, although these can be less than what they appear to be. One new arrival signed up for the Thursday evening gathering of the Gitmo Swingers and discovered the only fun the Swingers are into is square dancing.

As would be expected in such a climate, Gitmo offers the greatest variety of recreation outdoors: tennis, archery, horseback riding, football, softball, soccer—virtually all the popular sports. The minimal cost is also attractive. For only four dollars, for example, Gitmoites can play eighteen holes of golf. The course, which is kept up by thirty thousand gallons of water a day, is reminiscent of eighteen tiny oases in a desert. Golfers cope with the aid of Gitmo rolls: strips of Astro Turf carried in golf bags and put down on the dry fairways between the putting greens.

There is even a hunting season, though short, during which hunters can bag deer, dove, pigeon, and other birds. Hunters must be accompanied by a volunteer game warden.

For those who prefer their animals alive, a small children's zoo contains a few goats, donkeys, iguanas, and banana rats—or at least

The golf course and housing units on a hazy morning

The iguana is one of seven animal species protected at Gitmo.

the cages for them. The base abounds in more fascinating types of birds and animals, but the zoo is a place children can go for an outing. It is surrounded by playground equipment, picnic tables, and barbecue grills.

As the zoo suggests, kids and their needs are not overlooked. The little people have three parks as well as playgrounds throughout the family housing areas. Organized youth activities include the traditional Boy Scouts and Girl Scouts.

Because of Gitmo's location, water sports are the star attraction for everyone. The translucent waters, profuse with crustaceans, coral, and fish of myriad iridescent colors, project a paradise for skin divers—perhaps the only slice of paradise Gitmo has to offer. The water is so clean and clear that the ocean floor appears to be inches away when it actually may be twenty feet below.

Danger is also deceptive, lurking not far away. Swimmers are cautioned to put on some type of shoes to protect their feet from sea urchins and coral while wading and not to wear anything shiny that might attract such predators as barracudas and sharks. There has never been a shark attack, fortunately, but this fact hasn't prevented shark stories as wild as any sea story spun by a sailor or the producers of *Jaws*.

Bathers who prefer the bay-side beaches must keep to areas that are dredged and pooled-in to protect them from the powerful undertow and swift current there. Any swimming outside of the enclosed tidal pools must be done while wearing a buoyancy-control device, commonly used for snorkeling and diving.

Perils notwithstanding, the beaches are a big draw on weekends and holidays, as evidenced by the beer and soda can tabs strewn in the sand—"just like home," as John put it. Many beaches have the additional lure of cabanas, picnic tables, and grills. But military personnel must be particularly careful of sunburn; they can receive disciplinary action if a sunburn keeps them from duty.

Some beaches, like other things on a military base, are restricted to certain groups. Cuzco Beach, for example, is for base personnel only, even though it has no protective swimming area. This means that visiting ships' crews are verboten; they have their own strip of sand, Cable Beach, next door. Cuzco has a special designation because it is a conservation preserve. Shells, fish, and coral are not allowed to be removed from this scenic area.

Sailboats, skiffs, other small boats, and power boats for water skiing are available for a few dollars an hour. And Gitmo boasts its

Windmill Beach, for enlisted personnel

own yacht club, which conducts races nearly every week.

All boats are required to fly the United States flag so they can be readily identified. Gitmo may be as isolated as an island, but even islands are vulnerable to an encompassing sea. In 1970, for instance, three Haitian Coast Guard vessels pulled into the bay after they had fired on their capital, Port-au-Prince. The Haitians requested asylum and were escorted to Puerto Rico. Today, through the Haitian Interdiction Program, the Navy attempts to head off Haitian refugees before they arrive.

In addition to Cubans fleeing Cuba, there are Cubans trying to get back into their country, using Gitmo as a jumping-off point as those in the Bay of Pigs invasion did. In 1981, a minuscule exile group called Cubans United attempted a peaceful invasion of the base. They hoped to land three thousand unarmed men at a canal near the base and establish an anti-Castro government in exile at Gitmo.

The Cubans United got their idea after a report in the *Washington Star* claimed the Reagan Administration was considering filling Gitmo with unwanted Cuban exiles and then giving the base back to Cuba. (Are former Gitmo JO's working for the *Star?*) Curiously, the Cuban group's military advisor, Frank A. Sturgis, was one of those convicted of the break-in of the Watergate building during the Nixon Administration.

Gitmo braced for the invasion by building a barbed-wire compound as a holding area adjacent to the Marine Corps Lyceum. The CO announced that anybody arriving uninvited would be arrested.

Undeterred, the ambitious Cubans sailed from Miami, where they had been living. After they became shipwrecked on Providenciales Island, they had to be rescued by the United States, at considerable cost.

Although the press dubbed it "Mission Implausible," the venture wasn't any stunt. One of the leaders was a veteran of the Bay of Pigs disaster in which his seventeen-year-old son was killed. He was quoted after the Gitmo failure as saying: "If there were another invasion, I'd go tomorrow. It's because of my son. And then, the

Cubans say that a man who doesn't love his country doesn't love his mother."

The Cuban Government, consequently, has good reason to suspect any boats approaching from the Naval base, even though the attacking craft may only be recreational boats off course. Such was the case in 1979 when a schoolteacher and female petty officer sailed from the base up the Guantánamo River into Cuban territory. A Marine guard tried to stop them, but they kept going and the Cubans captured them. Although the pair were released, the Special Services boat was returned only after efforts by the United States' diplomatic envoy in Havana.

In 1981, four sailors from the crew of the visiting U.S.S. *Raleigh* also strayed too far. After sailing their two rental boats beyond the Water Gate, they were waved off by Cuban guards, who fired a warning shot across the bow of one of the boats before taking the sailors into custody. The Cubans detained them in Boquerón, then transferred them to Havana where they were turned over to the United States Special Interest Section.

When the four returned to Gitmo, they were "dealt with promptly," and liberty was canceled for all their shipmates on the *Raleigh*. It's easy to imagine how popular they must have been for the rest of that cruise.

Most Gitmo boaters stay safely in the bay on board one of the rental craft or on a "Barrel Boat," the floating equivalent of the

```
Help!  I'm leaving and my barrel
boat needs a good home, TLC, and
a little work.  Comes with extras
up the yazoo.  12x24.  40HP Johnson
electric start that needs to be
hooked up.  Battery charger, head,
flares, life jackets, storage
space, three gas tanks, rigged for
fishing with pole holders every-
where you turn.  I've got $1600
in it, make me an offer.  Hurry!
Please!  Call 2155 AWH.
```

Classified ad for a barrel boat

Gitmo Special. These popular boats, used for fishing and pleasure, vary in size but not in construction: a platform floating on barrels welded together. Base personnel usually build them or buy one from someone departing for another duty station. Barrel Boats often have roofs, sun decks, and a decor to match the owner's taste, which is often pretty ghastly.

The most prized recreation, however, is not at Gitmo at all. It's known locally as getting off the Rock. Space is often available for residents on planes or ships traveling to such Caribbean vacation spots as Jamaica, Puerto Rico, Haiti, and the Dominican Republic. Another option is to catch a flight to Norfolk, although it isn't always easy to find a seat, even if you're willing to pay the regular fare. Standby seating, for which a ten-dollar processing fee is charged, is even more difficult, especially during the summer and holidays.

Following the outdoor movie, John took me to the Barrel Club for a nightcap. "They say you can't afford not to drink at Gitmo," he said. "But I'm not sure if that's because booze is duty free or because you're likely to go nuts if you don't drink."

To cover both possibilities, we each ordered the popular rum and Coke.

At the opposite end of the well-stocked bar, I noticed our barracks MAA eating a slice of pizza with his beer.

"Their best customer," John observed. "I think he spends every night here. Takes his meals here. I wouldn't be surprised if they buried him here."

I turned away, preferring to watch the men playing table shuffleboard in the center of the crowded room, which bordered on an equally packed open-air patio.

When the club closed, we flowed with the mob up the hill to the barracks, pooled in light under the palms. I thanked John for his base tour and told him I was turning in.

"But you haven't seen the star attraction, yet."

I asked what he meant, but he only laughed, saying, "You'll see."

I couldn't imagine what he wanted to show me at that time of night. Although we had late duty passes, curfew was in effect and security would be stopping anybody who looked like two sailors out after hours.

In the AFRTS section of the barracks, John demanded the keys to the pickup that he had relinquished to two other JO's before dinner.

"Where are you going?" the keeper of the keys wanted to know.

"Visiting," John said.

"Who?"

"Some friends."

"I didn't know you had any."

"That shows how much you know, cactus puss."

"Well, then, enlighten us," the other journalist demanded, clutching the keys in his fist.

The more John maintained our after-hours foray was of no interest to them, the more intrigued they became and the more determined to tag along.

"Why not let them?" I asked, trying to mediate. I couldn't understand what difference it made.

"You'll be sorry," John promised. He looked as disgusted with me as if I had told him the chief and I had become the best of shipmates. Maybe that's why John made me sit in the back of the pickup with the previous driver when the four of us left the barracks.

"What's up?" my fresh-air companion asked as we drove down the barracks fire lane.

"I honestly don't know. I guess it's a surprise."

As either luck or John would have it, we got behind a "Smoky Joe," the insect-control truck, inching along like an overgrown beetle as it blasted mosquito-breeding areas on the roadside with yellow clouds of pesticide. We pounded on the window and cursed John, but he merely shrugged and turned up his hands, pantomiming: What am I supposed to do about it?

Turning onto Sherman Avenue, we left the bug truck behind, the street lamps casting an eerie light on its sulfuric cloud.

When we approached a group of duplex houses overlooking the golf course, my companion shouted, "I know where we're going!"

and rubbed his hands in Dickensian glee.

We're going to the brig, I whispered to myself.

"This is the teachers' quarters," he enlightened me. "WOMEN!"

Then I was convinced we would end up in the brig.

As John jumped out and rushed to the door, I could picture myself among the head-shaven prisoners riding in the back of the dump truck that carried them to chop weeds or pick up trash along the roadsides. Since boot camp, I knew I didn't look good in short hair.

A pretty young woman about our age opened the door and John somehow convinced her that we should be asked in. Hanging back in case we had to make a run for it, I couldn't hear all of the exchange.

When we entered the living room, which was furnished like an inexpensive motel, another young teacher rushed out of the room with an armload of undergarments.

Undeterred, John introduced us. Our unflappable hostess smiled pleasantly, possibly repressing laughter, and asked if she could get us something to drink: a needless question.

When she went to the kitchen, I jerked my head toward the door, but John looked at me with deeply puzzled eyes. A quick glance at our companions revealed no help there. They had already gone into labored breathing.

Momentarily, our hostess returned with glasses of beer. Her two curious roommates followed.

We stood like proper gentlemen and went through the introductions again.

We sat down and attempted chat, the conversation sputtering. I felt as if we were four goonie birds courting three reluctant hens.

Before very long we heard a knock at the door. All heads, goonies and hens, craned in that direction as our hostess, wondering aloud who that could possibly be, opened the door to three impressive Marines, led by an energetic young captain seemingly ready to take on San Juan, if not Bulkeley, Hill.

We stood and did the introduction ritual once more. And then there were eight goonie birds dancing around.

Quickly the "grunts" maneuvered the women to one side of the room, excommunicating us from the conversation as effectively as if they had brought the fence line along with them.

Since it was evident even to John that we didn't have a hope of conquest, we finished our beers, excused ourselves, and showed ourselves out the door.

Outside, we really gave it to the Marine Corps.

"What do they see in those grunts?"

"Who invited them, anyway?"

"The same person who invited us," John replied. "Nobody."

One of our companions wanted to vent his anger by ramming the house with the truck. John convinced him it wasn't practical, and we took our deflated egos back to the barracks where they belonged.

Fortunately for the unmarried men at Gitmo today, it's a little easier to get a date. A few teachers and nurses aren't the only unattached women on the base. As mentioned before, the first unmarried service women arrived in 1972. The women are assigned to the same jobs at Gitmo as they would have on any Naval base, including operating radar, repairing tugboats, maintaining pay records, and even staffing AFRTS. They are not assigned to the Marine Ground Defense Force.

Nine

"I'D like to see you up front." It was the chief's voice, calling from the intercom box on the concrete wall behind the long brown drapes that had survived *Cooking with the Commander*.

Worried that the word of the previous evening's escapade was out, I walked up the long passageway to the office area.

To my relief, the chief was in a buoyant mood.

"I've got an outstanding idea," he began as I entered his office. "We're going to produce a documentary." When I failed to inquire about the subject, his self-satisfied smile sagged. Exasperation crept into his confident tone.

"On fleet training. It's so obvious, we've overlooked it," he insisted, and reasoned why we, the Gitmo public affairs unit, should undertake such a project. "Gitmo's Fleet Training Group plays a crucial role in the defense of the United States, but how many people know about it?" He envisaged great success for a twenty-minute featurette, distributed to movie houses as a short subject. After it's initial run, the film would be released for television.

I thought he was deluded if he actually believed what he said. Surely the boost such a project would give his chances for promotion had clouded his judgment. In my opinion, a commercial film on Gitmo's Fleet Training Group, however deserving FTG might be, wouldn't sell even if *Playboy* bunnies infiltrated the staff. I didn't argue, however, choosing instead to duck out by claiming I already had more work than I could handle.

"Is that all that's bothering you?" The chief laughed. "What do you think you have a crew back there for? You're a department head. You're not supposed to do all the work yourself. Get those slackers off their duffs."

Feeling trapped, I asked who would work on the project.

"We'll write it and get the photo lab to shoot it. Just leave the arrangements to me."

I pleaded for John's help. The chief eyed me suspiciously, considering whether I intended to sabotage his dream. Regardless of what he thought of John, however, he couldn't deny his ability.

"All right," he relented. "But I have a feeling I'll regret this."

The next hurdle was to convince John. I anticipated a flat rejection, but he surprised me, saying, "Well, why not? It'll get us out of this tomb for awhile. And maybe we can do something a little creative for a change."

I assumed that boredom and lethargy had pacified his animosity toward the chief. I should have known better.

With a rough outline of the subject matter to be covered, John and I met the chief at the fleet landing on the appointed morning. Because he hadn't seen the photographers arrive, his tonsils were in a knot. He paced along the pier, chewing his cigar. "Where are they? I told them to be here by 0-five-hundred!"

"We can't wait any longer," the boatswain in charge told us. "Are you coming with us or not?"

"I guess we'll have to use the photographers on the ship," the chief decided. Despite the cool morning, he was perspiring heavily. He squinted through the dim light at the road behind us one last time. "Anyone dumb enough to miss the boat would have missed the action, anyway."

Clutching our 35-mm cameras, we joined the shadowy figures in the motor whaleboat and headed toward the aircraft carrier.

Each year at Gitmo, seventy-five to one hundred ships of the

A motor whaleboat takes Fleet Training Group (FTG) instructors to a ship for the day's training exercise.

Atlantic Fleet, occasionally including icebreakers, participate in maneuvers that last three to seven weeks. The "School for Ships" is mandatory for all ships that are either newly commissioned, recently overhauled, or in need of intensive refresher training. Allies of the United States have also used Gitmo's school, which employs a staff of 150—a figure that may rise as the United States moves closer toward its goal of a 600-ship Navy.

The FTG approach is called "whole-ship training," which means the entire ship is involved in the various exercises, not single departments one at a time. It's a highly intensive course, based on a "worst-case" philosophy.

Waves slapped against the bottom of the launch as we chugged through the predawn light toward the aircraft carrier. In a loud voice the chief began to lecture us on the elements of good photography, a briefing intended to impress the instructors in the boat. Whenever he paused, I attempted to drown him out with a cover-up conversation. But John refused to cooperate: he wanted to give the chief a wide berth to wreck himself.

Steadily the aircraft carrier grew from Lilliputian to Gulliverian size, its flight deck looming ten stories over us like a massive arch. In the bobbing launch underneath, I worried that we might capsize

The aircraft carrier U.S.S. *America*

before everyone could leap to the floating platform beside the keel and climb the ladder to the ship.

When we stood up to wait our turn, we discovered the photographers with grins on their faces as wide as two Cheshire cats confident they could take on a rat. They had been sitting in the group of men behind the chief throughout the trip. Their victim smiled sickly, suggesting he wanted to claim he had been joking but knew that excuse wouldn't float. For once the cat, as they say, had his tongue.

In an attempt to disassociate ourselves from the chief, John and I scrambled up the swaying ladder faster than we would have dared otherwise.

We wandered the honeycombed passageways of the enormous iron belly. Tired, dungaree-clad men with stained hands and exhausted pools around their eyes stared at us in our crisp white uniforms.

"How are we suppose to 'blend in with the action'?" John wanted to know. "Dressed like this we look like two boot camp graduates on their first liberty."

I reminded him that I had told the chief our sparkling white tropical uniforms would be inappropriate. Since the chief should have known that, I concluded he aimed to try to impress.

John agreed with my assessment, adding, "I could kick myself for letting you talk me into this."

We took our time finding the operations control room, which our leader had summarily dubbed the press headquarters. When we opened the hatch and stepped over the metal frame into the room, we found him holding forth, waving his cigar like a semaphore, among a group of chief petty officers, the "backbone of the Navy," as our AFRTS vertebra was fond of saying.

To us, he said, "Glad to see you men found your way. I'll make sailors out of you, yet."

I immediately announced my departure to shoot some stills for fillers and transitional material.

"Good man. I'm on my way down to the CPO mess to get some firsthand observations. Meet you on the flight deck later," the chief said. "And what are you doing?" he asked John.

John squeezed out a saccharine smile, saying, "I thought I'd see what the Old Man has to say."

116

"I don't think that would—"

"Only joshin', Chief."

Looking like tourists with cameras slung on our shoulders, John and I went down to the flight deck where the base photographers told us in unpublishable language that they didn't want us doing their job.

"I could get some material for transition and slides, which would leave you free for mo-pic work," I offered.

"We don't need any JO's help."

Although I had learned something about photography at my previous duty station, the Naval Schools of Photography where they had received their training, I decided not to push the issue. I had enough work waiting for me back at the TV station.

During the first exercise on the typical first day of training, the FTG instructors grade the ship's performance in navigating a narrow channel under simulated conditions of low visibility, followed by sailing through a simulated minefield on the way out of the harbor.

At sea, the ship begins drills that include various types of navigation, surface-to-air gunnery practice, engineering casualty control, underway replenishment, general quarters, and anti-subma-

FTG instructor Richard Thomas, center, evaluates fire-hose teams during shipboard drills below decks.

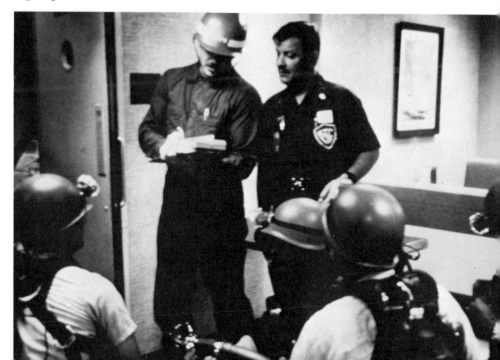

rine warfare. The FTG instructors evaluate the crew's performance after each exercise.

Aircraft carrier training differs because of the huge scope of the job. As many as six thousand men and shipboard aircraft operations are involved. The training period is shorter and more intense. A detachment of instructors usually boards the big ship in its home port in order to conduct training en route to Gitmo.

As our carrier glided past the Leeward Point airfield, one of the ship's journalists arrived to serve as our guide.

We waited there on the flight deck. Like a football field swept by a strong breeze, the ship tilted slowly up and down, rhythmically changing the horizon from sky to sea, sea to sky. Not until I looked back at Gitmo did I realize the extent of the ship's motion. I watched fascinated while the brown hilly island appeared and disappeared beyond the edge of the flight deck as if the ship, not the land, were the stable object.

"I think the fish are in for some Gitmo chow," John said, holding his stomach.

"Haven't we been embarrassed enough?"

Suddenly a siren blared, and John forgot about his queasiness as the sailors scrambled.

"General quarters! General quarters!" bleated out of the intercom system.

Even though we knew the drill was only practice, it produced a sobering, chilling feeling. We shrank back out of the way of the clamor as VC-10 Skyhawks started their simulated air raid.

Bandaged sailors soon arrived and took up positions as mock victims, injured or dead, on the flight deck. With their bandages stained to simulate blood, they looked surprisingly authentic.

"They don't look like they should be out of sick bay," John snickered in my ear. I was relieved he had apparently forgotten about his stomach.

When the siren sounded again, medical teams and stretcher bearers raced on deck to remove the casualties. Next, men in rubber suits emerged and began scrubbing down the areas of the deck marked as contaminated by nuclear, biological, or chemical agents.

During simulated crash-and-fire drills, an "injured" man is secured to a stretcher on the flight deck while men in protective suits lead a fire-fighting team toward a "burning" aircraft.

They worked in such earnest that I couldn't help looking down at my nicely polished shoes to see if any of the deadly agents had gotten on them.

Sometimes general quarters during a training exercise becomes the real thing when accidents occur. Ships have run aground, into piers, and into one another. In 1974, an explosion on the submarine U.S.S. *Jallao* sent nineteen injured sailors to Gitmo's hospital for treatment.

After the "above decks" drill, John and I followed our escort, winding down ladders until we arrived in the engine room during "air-tight integrity." The faces of the crew were unforgettable. They looked stunned, shocked, fighting for survival like divers out of oxygen. Sweat soaked their hair and dunagrees, water dripped from their faces as if they had become one with the overhead pipes.

How were we supposed to glorify this picture of hell: fires red behind the screens of the boiler doors, steam hissing from all directions? The young sailors checking the temperature gauges and pipes eyed us in our implacable whites. I couldn't have felt more out of place if I had come from another solar system.

After a brief explanation of what was happening in the engine room, our escort led us up the ladder out of that raging inferno. He took us to the Damage Control Center where junior officers and senior petty officers waited at control panels encircling a huge lieutenant commander. Drenched in sweat, the commander was perched on a swivel chair in the center like a sumo wrestler about to grapple with the controls.

Before the next event, John and I stood drip-drying on the flight deck. The trade winds whipped our trousers against our legs.

"I'll take Gitmo over this any day," I said.

"It's not always this bad on board," John reminded me. "Don't forget this is a second boot camp. Everything will be different when this is over."

"Yes. Especially if they get transferred to Gitmo."

We stayed for a time, watching the escorting ships practice firing their weapons at targets, including those towed by VC-10. Other exercises were going on, too, of course.

When we walked inside, I asked John if he intended to eat.

"You're becoming a real comedian."

"Sorry. I forgot."

I found the galley on my own.

Waiting in a long line, I scanned the tired, greasy faces and imagined what a smaller prison than Gitmo would be like.

I eventually moved up to the rack of silverware and metal trays. Feeling as if I were in the Gitmo enlisted mess hall, I moved along in front of the steam table and scooped up the familiar food before the interrogating eyes of the sweat-slicked cooks.

After weaving through the herd carrying metal trays, I found a place at one of the long, narrow tables. When I sat down, I was confronted by the depleted face of a young sailor eating his food in an abstract manner that suggested it was merely one aspect of the day's routine. I studied his face between bites of food: it created the impression of lost time, of wasted youth.

I waited for an opportunity to speak to him. I particularly wanted to know why he looked as if he had been wound up tight and let go too many times, although that was the kind of personal question

I didn't dare ask. I could only surmise.

Finally, I plunged ahead: "You been aboard long?"

He looked up hesitantly, unsure he had been spoken to. In some ways he reminded me of Guber, especially his brown hair parted and combed neatly except for the rooster tail at the back. He, too, had oily skin blemished with the anxieties and hormones of adolescence, frightened brown eyes, and a mouth half-open as if he had trouble breathing.

"How long have you been on board?" I repeated.

"Three months," he managed before the fork delivered in another load of roast beef and mashed potatoes, the main stay of the Navy.

"What do you do?"

"I work in the laundry." He chewed and cut another chunk of beef.

My stomach knotted as I pictured hour after hour in a hot room permeated with perspiration. It recalled the jobs I had during school days, washing dishes and scrubbing kitchens in restaurants. Suddenly my roast beef reminded me of cleaning meat saws.

Concentrating on his food, the sailor said, "Oh, it isn't so bad. Somebody's got to do it. I've issued linen and cleaned compartments, too. But maybe after this cruise I'll get a school."

"Doesn't it bother you?"

"What?"

"Working in the laundry all day."

"I don't think about it. Griping only makes it worse." He looked up at my grimace. "It's not as bad as all that. Once you get into the routine, it gets easier. People begin to know you. When the officers want their pants pressed, they ask for me. It's good. I have lots of friends now." He stopped short with the sudden embarrassment of someone who believed he had said too much.

We ate in silence for awhile; then he asked, "Have you been ashore yet? What's it like?"

"I'm stationed there. So it doesn't hold much attraction for me. But the beaches are nice," I added to give him something to look forward to when he had pressed enough pants to get liberty.

"How come you're all duded up?"

"I work at the TV station. We're doing a documentary film about fleet training—at least, we're trying to."

"Wow! How'd you get that kinda assignment?"

"It was somewhat of an accident."

When I continued eating, he said, "Well, I gotta get back." He got up awkwardly and edged his way out between the row of hunched backs and lifting arms, his rooster tail disappearing in the wake of my depression.

When I finished, I strolled the deck for some fresh air and looked at the topside crew curled up next to anything that formed shelter from the wind. Their heads flopping to the side like dead chickens, mouths agape, the sailors sought twenty minutes of peace during the lunchtime respite.

John and our escort arrived shortly. Although I was curious about where John had been, I didn't ask.

We made our way up to the bridge to watch the flight operations.

When we stepped out of the last hatch, the chief saw us and motioned us over. Leaning against a stanchion, he pointed to the television camera mounted above us.

"They've got video tape," he mouthed against the wind. "Every flight is filmed. In case of an accident, they can figure out what caused it." He shook his head in appreciation. "We sure could use something like that at the station."

"I think our mistakes are evident enough," John cracked.

Looking as if he had eaten something disagreeable, the chief returned to watching the teams of men, distinguished by vests of different bright colors, working to ready the Phantoms for takeoff.

Coaxed by the crews, the swept-wing jets lined up one after the other, creating an angled row of skulls and crossbones painted in black on tall silver tails. We watched in awe as the jets roared off, circled, and returned to the ship where a hook on a cable stretched across the deck snapped them to a halt. I realized then that my pre-service ambition of becoming a jet pilot had been ludicrous. I knew I could no more land a jet on an aircraft carrier than leap off

Training exercises include refueling at sea.

a tall building with a cape around my neck.

So far, John and I had watched drills for nuclear, biological, and chemical attack, damage control, and various air operations.

The final event of that day, which I suppose might be included in the seamanship category, was replenishment at sea. For this exercise, an ammunition ship pulled alongside the carrier like a playful dolphin riding the waves thrown out by the bigger ship. On both vessels, men rushed to form lines of rope handlers for the admiral's trip on the yellow high-line chair between the two ships; others waited for supplies which would go across further amidships.

We hurried to the open hangar bay, below the flight deck, to watch the Old Man, in an attempt to make the exercise realistic, ride across the perilous gap. He climbed in the chair. A couple of the supervisors checked the seat buckles. Then the line of sailors behind the chair and an equal number on the other ship strained as they pulled on the ropes, lifting the admiral up and over the side.

Throughout the drill, the petty officer in charge proudly called out the commands: crisp, sharp, loud enough for all to hear. Did this give the admiral confidence in that precarious, free-swinging chair bobbing along above the churning sea? I wondered.

"Do you think we could get the chief to take a ride in that chair?" John asked me.

"If he thought it would help his chances for promotion."

"Maybe we could volunteer him for the man overboard drill."

"They already have a dummy for that."

As if summoned, the chief walked up with his cup of coffee and smiled his approval of the sailors' endeavor. Those in the vicinity looked curious to know who the celebrity was. Somebody from Washington?

"This is the kind of thing we want," the chief pointed out to us. "This is the *real* Navy. That"—he indicated the strong, young petty officer proudly shouting the commands—"is the mark of a Navy man."

"Sure, Chief," John agreed in a tone reminiscent of Ski's. "Look what it did for you."

The chief laughed, teeth snapping the air. Quickly, though, he slurped away the *ha, ha, ha*'s with a lick of his tongue.

"I hope you'll be happy in your work at the boat shed," I told John.

Safely on the ammunition ship, the admiral prepared to tempt fate again.

After the replenishment, the chief ushered us up to the bridge for the daily postmortem. When we arrived at the wardroom, the chief opened the first hatch and barged in on the creche of brass as if they were his TV crew. The senior officers shot us the death stare.

John and I shrank back as the chief bowled his way forward, saying, "Oh, don't let us disturb you. I'm just showing my young journalists here where the decision making goes on. We want all of you to be in the film, of course. That's good just the way you are."

The ship's admiral blinked in disbelief and, seeming tongue-tied by the absurd situation, ignored us and continued listening to the critique of the FTG instructors.

I backed farther into the corner, but the chief followed and started whispering and pointing. In terror I watched the admiral's face harden until it looked as if it could have been added to Mount Rushmore.

A young lieutenant quickly swept us out of the compartment, and before long we were on the launch back to the island.

The chief, however, remained undaunted. Turning to the photographers, who were once again seated behind us, he offered his peace pipe: "Get some good stuff?"

"Not bad for missing the boat."

The chief laughed good-naturedly, sacrificing his pride for better public relations. "Come on, boys, we all put our foot in it once in awhile."

"Yes," John interjected. "It's called foot and mouth disease."

The chief attempted a retort: "And I thought we left Ski at home."

When we reached the Gitmo boat landing, the chief again thanked the photographers and praised them loudly in front of the other men getting off the launch. The photographers walked away, cutting him short.

"Well, how do you like that?" he asked us.

With my foot I pressed John's toes, threatening him if he answered.

John withdrew his foot and asked, "Is tomorrow a replay? Same time, same place?"

"There's no need to go back. You've seen enough to get the feel. It's mostly repetitive from now on. If the photographers need more footage, they can make their own arrangements."

"Good idea, Chief."

I hurried John away.

Ten

WHEN the fleet training footage had been processed and delivered to the station, the chief announced, "I think I'm going to write the script myself. I used to have quite a flare for writing before I got bogged down in administration."

His spontaneous idea smacked of careful rehearsal.

"What are you smirking at?" he asked John. "Don't you think I can do it?"

"Sure, chief. You can do anything you say you can."

Unsure whether John was being sarcastic, the chief decided to overlook the comment. "This is going to be outstanding!" he assured us, draining his coffee cup. "Outstanding!" he repeated and rushed back to his office to capture his new ideas.

John flashed me a murderous look. "I deserve this for letting you dupe me into it." He stalked out, leaving me foolishly holding the offending reel of film.

Thus began the long process of cutting and splicing the footage in a futile attempt to match it with the chief's narration. Both of us were novices who had never edited a film before. But the task was particularly arduous because our editing equipment consisted solely of an out-of-date splicer that glued together strips of film. To view a frame I had to hold it up to the light. I also had my usual TV work to do.

John refused to help and suggested I accidentally lose the film by substituting it for one of the TV programs in the weekly return shipment. The chief, meanwhile, badgered me to know when I would be finished. I stalled, reminding him that quality movies took a long time to produce. I was beginning to sound like our "Please Stand By" message and was running the risk of broadcasting it to a captive audience at the boat shed.

But then I was unexpectedly rescued. Guber heralded the event early one morning in the barracks.

"He's back. He's back! All hands meeting at 0-eight-hundred!" the radio DJ blared, shaking bunks. "Ski's coming with the van."

"Shut up!" nearby voices demanded.

"Will somebody turn him off?"

Guber didn't have to explain to us who he was talking about. Only one person could have caused such a fuss.

When we reached the station, we each took a folding chair and a cup of coffee and assembled in the TV studio. The chief sulked in with an operatic expression of suffering and victimization. He set up a chair off to one side.

The others waited, muttering, until the lieutenant opened the studio door.

Ski jumped up and shouted, "Attention on deck!" Ramrod stiff, he looked like a balding, portly tenor in *H.M.S. Pinafore*.

"Seats, gents!" the lieutenant snapped as he marched through the middle of us and took up a position leaning against the news desk. He was tall and trim, with the clean-cut Ivy League appearance of so many junior officers in the Navy who seemed to be turned out of the same mold. Holding us in suspense, he smiled with a mouth so wide it looked stretched as he slowly scanned the scurrilous faces before him. He appeared to have enough glistening white teeth to make the *Guinness Book of World Records*.

"It's good to get off the Rock for awhile. You can go bananas around here." His little joke, as Ski was fond of saying, was received as enthusiastically as another year at Gitmo.

Undaunted, the lieutenant tried again: "It's good to be back. I've lost my suntan." He paused for the laughter, but it had not been properly cued. And despite the waves of virulence pulsating from his audience, he kept smiling, a meretricious smile that seemed to have served as the chief's model.

"Before we get down to business," he said, "I thought you might like to see some slides of my trip. It was fantastic!" Pushing the table away, he stood to the side of a portable screen. "Are the slides ready?"

"Aye, aye, sir," Guber sang out from the rear of the studio.

Teeth clenched, eyes narrowed, the crew slid down in their chairs and folded their arms.

When the ordeal ended, the lieutenant hiked up his carefully pressed pants and sat on the edge of the table. He cleared his throat as his smile soured into a look of stern authority.

"As you should all recall, I made it perfectly clear when I left here that there were to be no changes whatsoever in our operating procedures. Yet, I hardly get off the plane before various staff officers are commenting on the changes that have transpired in my absence. It seems the chief has had a phenomenal amount of initiative."

He paused for the snide chuckles he had solicited.

"I haven't yet determined what disciplinary measures need to be taken around here," the lieutenant continued. "First, I want to have a meeting of departmental heads at fifteen hundred to discuss—what shall we call it?—recent history?"

He was answered by silent contempt.

"All right, gents. That's all."

Ski jumped up and shouted "Attention on deck!" again as the lieutenant marched out.

Grumbling and cursing, the crew returned their chairs to the stack in the corner.

A short time later, the lieutenant called me into his office: an office much the same as the chief's, with a large executive desk flanked by the United States and Navy flags. The walls, however, were covered with pictures of the lieutenant smiling with senior officers at various types of military activities.

"I've heard about the good job you've done during your short time here, particularly in your good judgment," he began. "That's why I've decided to keep you on as TV department head."

"Thank you, sir," I said, wondering whom he could have been talking to.

"And you won't have to worry any longer about the chief's little project. Send the footage back to the photo lab and have them forward it to the Naval Photographic Center for storage." Pulling open his top desk drawer, he extracted a large film canister. "This is a new project for you. It's some footage taken of . . ."

With his pet project under my arm, I returned to the studio, having learned a lesson: lieutenants had promotions to worry about, too.

Before I had time to finish the lieutenant's film, however, fate again intervened, this time in the form of the Bureau of Naval Personnel. Hermes, temporarily disguised as our yeoman, delivered the news one evening while I was helping to set up for our live shows.

Ski sashayed into the studio and announced, "I hope you like penguins."

"Is that a dinner invitation?" I asked, trying to ignore him.

"No, silly," he giggled, flapping my orders in the air. "You're going to the South Pole!"

The crew laughed, but I didn't. I realized I had been picked up for Antarctic duty, more than a year after I had volunteered for it. I had forgotten about it.

"You can refuse it, you know, and stay with us," Ski reminded me.

I looked around at the faces of the crew. "No. I'll think I'll take it."

"Chicken," Ski said.

In a few weeks, I departed Gitmo, transferring from one isolation to another, with the major difference being the climate. But that, as they say, is another story.

Appendix A

DISCOVERY

Christopher Columbus discovered *La Bahía de Guantánamo* on his second voyage to the New World. Looking for gold, he landed at what is now Fisherman's Point and spent the night of April 30, 1494. The next day, because he didn't find any prospect of riches, he left what he called *Puerto Grande*, after threatening to cut out the tongues of his crew if they didn't swear they had reached the Asian mainland, which was the aim of the voyage.

In the days of Spain's colonization of Latin America, Gitmo was often a haven for pirates. Cutthroats made it their base of operations for preying on ships sailing through the Windward Passage. At other times, the bay provided a refuge for ships from the frequent hurricanes in the West Indies.

BRITISH BASE

The British used the bay, which they renamed Cumberland Harbor, in 1741 as a base from which to attack the Spanish at Santiago de Cuba. The conflict was one of many disputes concerning trade in the New World between what were then the two world superpowers.

Among the British troops, incidentally, was the remnant of an American colonial regiment in which Lawrence Washington, the older half brother of George Washington, served. Lawrence later named the family estate Mount Vernon after the commander of the expedition, Vice Admiral Edward Vernon.

Staging from Guantánamo Bay, the British forces succeeded in reaching Guantánamo City without meeting any resistance. But they became bogged down, and yellow fever devastated the army of 3400.

In the meantime, Admiral Vernon had blockaded both Santiago and Guantánamo Bay. Again, yellow fever proved to be the actual enemy. More than two thousand troopers came down with it, and the debilitating disease also spread to the sailors, forcing the British to call off the expedition.

For the next century and a half, Gitmo languished in obscurity, unimportant and largely unwanted, despite its valuable harbor. With little fresh water in such a dry climate, only fishermen on the flat beach below the thirty-foot cliffs of Fisherman's Point and a few cattle ranchers on nearby grazing lands were willing to put up with the place.

Gitmo eventually gained some importance because of the sugar port of Caimanera on the western shore of the upper bay, five miles from the sea, and villagers from Fisherman's Point were employed to pilot ships up the bay to the port.

But it was war—the Spanish-American War of 1898—that once again brought men to Gitmo and Gitmo to prominence.

THE SPANISH-AMERICAN WAR

When Cubans began overt rebellion against oppressive Spanish rule in 1895, Spain rushed in 200,000 troops to defend the island. A decline in the United States' purchase of sugar, Cuba's primary source of income, set off a depression that fueled the revolution. As this suggests, the United States was heavily involved in the island's affairs. About 83 percent of all Cuban exports went to its big northern neighbor, which also had investments totaling fifty million dollars on the island. Unauthorized military expeditions from the United States had failed to free Cuba from Spanish corruption. The United States had also tried many times to purchase the island.

Rebel violence in turn led to more repressive Spanish countermeasures. Cuban refugees in the United States spread exaggerated tales of the Spanish atrocities, which were reprinted and sensationalized by major U.S. newspapers that were waging their own fierce battle for increased circulation.

On February 15, 1898, a mysterious explosion sank the battleship U.S.S. *Maine* in Havana Harbor, killing 260 men. A Naval board later concluded that a submarine mine had wrecked the ship, which had been positioned in the bay to protect North American citizens and their property.

Spain was willing to make large concessions to avoid war, but this was not enough to appease the United States, which demanded that the Spanish withdraw from Cuba and recognize the island's independence. News-

131

U.S. warships shell Spanish position in the battle for Gitmo, 1898.

papers in the United States whipped up public support for armed intervention with such slogans as "Remember the *Maine*, to hell with Spain!" A new world power was beginning to flex its muscles.

Two months after the sinking, Congress authorized President William McKinley to use the Armed Forces to expel the Spanish from Cuba. Faced with retreat or fight, Spain declared war on April 24; the United States followed suit the next day.

The United States blockaded Havana harbor and chased the Spanish fleet to Santiago Bay, forty miles west of Gitmo. After bottling up the Spanish, Rear Admiral W. T. Sampson dispatched two ships to reconnoiter Guantánamo Bay for a naval base.

At the time, a Spanish blockhouse stood on McCalla Hill, overlooking Fisherman's Point. A Spanish fort on Cayo del Toro, a tiny island between the lower and upper parts of the bay, commanded the narrow channel leading to Caimanera, where a Spanish gunboat, the *Sandoval*, was based. To the north, seven thousand troops defended Guantánamo City, and a string of blockhouses guarded the rail line.

Arriving on June 6, the U.S.S. *Marblehead* used its big guns to clear the blockhouse and village at Fisherman's Point. The Spanish gunboat *Sandoval* sailed down the bay to counterattack but quickly retreated before the cruiser's big guns.

The United States force severed the communication cables connecting Cuba with Haiti (which had their terminus at Fisherman's Point), cutting off Cuba from communication with the rest of the world.

When six hundred Marines landed at Fisherman's Point on June 10, they burned the village huts and the remains of the blockhouse to avoid catching yellow fever. The Spanish had regrouped, positioning eight hundred soldiers at the Cuzco Well, two miles to the southeast. Sunk in the 1870's, the well was the only source of water in the parched countryside where a large number of goats grazed.

These Spanish troops soon inflicted the first United States casualties of the war when, on June 12, two Marine pickets on outpost duty were killed. Despite having a superior force, the Marines were unable to pursue the snipers because of the throny tangle of trees, underbrush and cactus.

Two more Marines were killed that night by enemy bullets that riddled the American camp.

On their third day at Gitmo, the Marines were reinforced by fifty Cubans schooled in guerrilla tactics. They went out in pairs and burned the brush and undergrowth, while the *Marblehead* moved down the coast and shelled the well site.

The Spanish attacked again at nightfall, killing two more of the Marines. With no hope of immediate reinforcements, the situation was becoming desperate for the Leathernecks, who were worn out after one hundred sleepless hours.

The next morning, one force of 160 Marines and 50 Cubans approached the Cuzco Well along the sea cliffs, while a small force of Marines advanced by an inland valley and the U.S.S. *Dolphin* bombarded from the sea.

To direct the ship's fire, Sergeant John Quick climbed to the top of a hill, exposing himself to enemy fire while he calmly semaphored instructions to the *Dolphin*. Sergeant Quick earned the Congressional Medal of Honor for this episode, which captured the imagination of the American public. (The Marine dining facility built as part of the Marine BEQ in 1975 is named for Sergeant Quick.)

The battle for the Cuzco Well was chronicled by reporters, including Stephen Crane on assignment for a New York newspaper. Crane also wrote about the skirmish in *Wounds in the Rain*. As if to return the compliment, the Navy named one of the nearby hills for Crane, who died at the age of twenty-eight from tuberculosis compounded by the recurrent malarial fever he had caught in Cuba.

Caught in the cross fire between the *Dolphin* and the Marines, the Spanish fled. Fifty-eight were killed and 150 wounded. Although eighteen were captured, most escaped. The American side suffered only four wounded and two Marines killed. After burning the Spanish headquarters, the Marines filled up the well.

The Spanish were so demoralized that they retreated all the way to

Guantánamo City, which left the Marines unmolested at their Fisherman's Point camp until August 5, 1898, when they were sent home.

During the skirmish at Cuzco Well, the Spanish had been reinforcing their forts on Cayo del Toro and at Caimanera. To take out the forts, Admiral Sampson sent three ships, the *Marblehead, Texas,* and *Yankee,* up the bay. They destroyed the buildings and drove the Spanish from their guns and trenches. After returning safely to the mouth of the harbor, the admiral learned that the buoys his ships had passed by were actually contact mines. A mine sweep revealed that the mines hadn't exploded because of mechanical faults and a healthy growth of barnacles on the contact levers.

With Guantánamo Bay successfully occupied, attention centered on the battle for Santiago, where an American expeditionary force of seventeen thousand men landed on June 22. The blockaded city consequently was cut off by both land and sea. Seven thousand Spanish troops at Guantánamo City, only forty miles away, were unaware of the dire situation. Communication cables had been cut, and Cuban insurgents, encouraged by the United States forces at Gitmo, maintained a tight ring around the city. Had the Guantánamo City force been able to rush to the rescue, the outcome of the war might have been different.

Santiago surrendered. The U.S. Navy forced the Spanish fleet out of the harbor and destroyed the ships.

Less than a week later (on July 21), the United States launched from Gitmo an invasion of Puerto Rico, five hundred miles to the east. About 3500 men sailed from the bay in the last major event of the war.

On August 12, the hostilities ended with the signing of a preliminary peace treaty. The United States secured independence for Cuba and possession of Puerto Rico, Guam, and the Philippines, for which the victor paid the vanquished twenty million dollars.

Although Cuba became independent, it was occupied by U.S. troops and administered by a military governor. The Platt Amendment of 1901, unilaterally attached to the Cuban constitution, gave the United States the right to oversee international commitments, dominate the economy, intervene in internal affairs, and lease Gitmo as a fueling station for visiting ships.

The military occupation restored peace to the strife-beset island and modernized services in a move to prepare Cuba for incorporation into the United States. The Americans built schools, roads, bridges, and sewers. They paved streets and deepened Havana Harbor. Soon, the administrators instituted North American economic, cultural, and educational systems, including a voting procedure designed to eliminate Blacks from political participation.

134

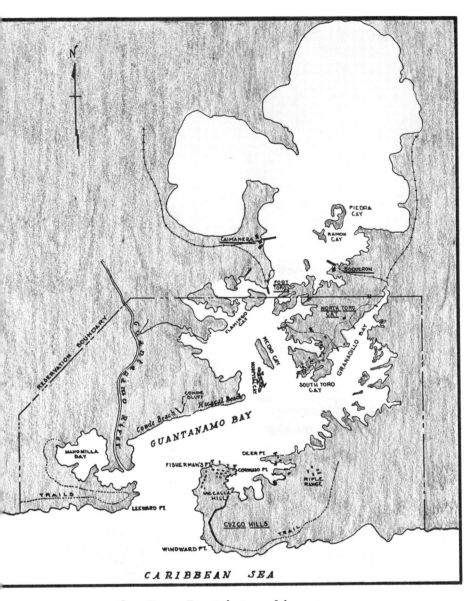

Guantánamo Bay at the turn of the century

FIRST COALING STATION

Construction was also underway at Gitmo, which Cuba formally turned over to the United States on December 10, 1903. Two tiny islands in the

135

Sharks foil first attempts at a floating dry dock.

upper bay, North Toro Cay and South Toro Cay, were selected as the site for the new naval station. One of the first projects was to join the two cays by building a road across the marshy flats, forming a connecting neck of land.

A wharf, ordnance piers, quarters, supply buildings, and a radio station were among the facilities started, while the personnel lived on a station ship and barges in the bay. Engineers began a large floating dry dock, but the project was soon abandoned due to the lack of funds and a problem with sharks entering the sealed-off pond through an underground water passage.

To the north, another revolution was brewing. This time the conflict was touched off when, in 1905, the first Cuban president, Estrada Palma, decided he didn't want to step down at the end of his first term. Residents recoiled at reports from Guantánamo City that described burnings, threatened atrocities, and cattle rustling. The station commandant organized a force to intervene, but his efforts proved unnecessary when United States troops once again poured in to restore order, including a Marine detachment of fifty men who proceeded from Gitmo to Guantánamo City.

The Marines pulled out after national elections in November of 1908 helped to appease the rebels. And two months later, the United States administrator handed over the Cuban Government to a newly chosen president.

By this time, several family quarters for officers had been built at Gitmo. Living conditions, however, remained shy of paradise. Friction sparked

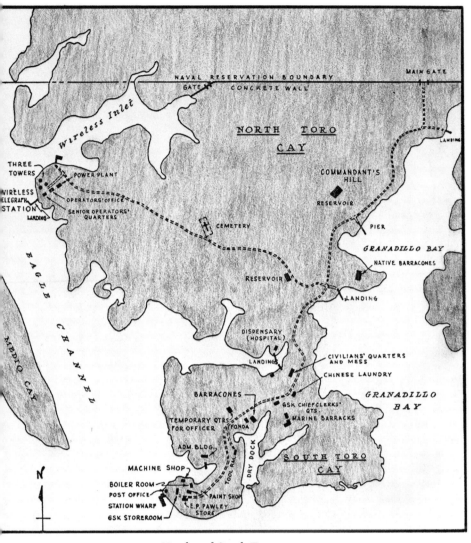

North and South Toro cays

among the families. One incident involved a pet goat that annoyed the station surgeon so much that he shot it with his rifle. When it appeared that Gitmo might have its own little war, the commandant decided to step in on the side of the Marine officer who owned the goat. Before the CO could act, however, he developed a cardiac condition the surgeon diagnosed as so serious that the CO had to be evacuated to the States. The prescribed treatment enabled the surgeon to escape disciplinary action,

137

and, not surprisingly, it cured the commandant. As soon as the CO arrived in Washington, D.C., his heart condition suddenly cleared up.

A desalination plant was erected on Hospital Cay in 1908, but the second-hand equipment was so worn out that it couldn't produce any acceptable water.

A much-needed general store was also opened—this on South Toro Cay, even though it violated the article of the lease agreement forbidding private enterprise on the reservation. As was often the case in those days, the proprietor was an American businessman; in this instance, one from Caimanera.

Congress and the Navy Department, however, weren't as sold on Gitmo as the Caimanera businessman. They put a hold on appropriations and ordered a survey in 1910 to find the most economical site for a new floating dry dock. Corinasco Cove, the present location of Gitmo's dockside, was picked because it offered the best protection from enemy attack.

RELOCATION AND EXPANSION

After cutting through mangroves on the steep shores of the ragged inlet, the civil engineering corps built storehouses, a power plant, oil tanks, a recreation field, and a target range. Low green bungalows for enlisteds were nestled in a tangle of palm and trumpet vines—"a flowery oasis in a desert of scrub and thorn"—along the cliff top above the inlet. For many years to follow, this would be called the "Main Station."

Before the new site was finished, another uprising in Cuba jangled Gitmo's nerves. This time it was a race war, sparked by the Afro-Cubans organizing to secure better jobs and more political patronage and to protest a law aimed at eliminating political associations based on color and race. The Marines were called in again to protect foreign nationals, primarily North Americans and their property. Meanwhile, Cuban troops squashed an uprising in Oriente Province (where Gitmo is located), killing three thousand Afro-Cubans.

On December 10, 1913, the relocated station was officially dedicated. That winter also marked the exit of the acting commandant. He was drummed out of the Navy after getting potted at a party held in his honor and ordering the station ship to fire a gun salute to him in the middle of the night.

During the period 1915-1918, Gitmo once again became the staging point for Marines sent to mediate in the affairs of Caribbean nations. In 1915, the Leathernecks moved through Gitmo to Haiti, which they occupied until 1934.

More Marines arrived at Gitmo in 1916. Their destination: the Domin-

Enlisted Men's Mess and Recreation Building,
1916, later became Chief Petty Officers' Mess.

ican Republic. After a decade of increased American presence, similar to
what had happened in Cuba, the Dominican Government had collapsed
and the United States had assumed complete control. Among other things,
the Marines created a modern military police force, an instrument by
which future Dominican strong men would seize power and dominate the
country.

Gitmo's Marine detachment, in addition to garrison responsibility on
the base, continued to support the units on duty in Haiti and the Dominican Republic until they were withdrawn.

By 1916, quarters for unaccompanied officers and enlisted men were
completed and the station's complement of two hundred men moved in.
As a further improvement on Gitmo living, the commandant started the
first vegetable farm. It was planted in the Cuzco Valley, near the present
Naval Cemetery, and was irrigated by water from the Cuzco Well, which
apparently had been excavated.

As though to keep Gitmo residents from becoming too complacent with
their new comforts, another civil war erupted in Cuba. It grew out of a
dispute between the two major political parties over the 1916 election.
The losers, the Liberal Party, revolted. After their supporters had captured Santiago, the American Consul requested a United States man-of-
war to maintain communication and allay the fears of the citizens. Gitmo's
CO, commander Dudley W. Knox, left his vegetable garden and volunteered the station ship, the *Petrel*.

Since the old *Petrel* was in pathetic condition, it was a feeble show of

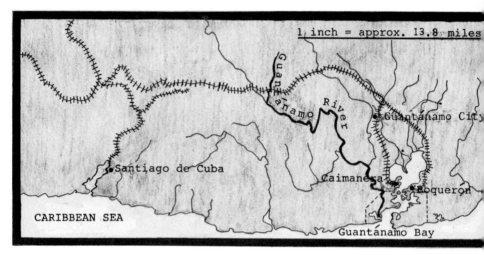

The southeastern coastal area of Cuba

power, but Knox succeeded in mediating the dispute. Exceeding his orders, he dissuaded the revolutionists from mining the harbor and the Federalists from attacking from the sea. Although neither side posed much of an actual threat, the citizens of Santiago were delighted with the temporary neutralization of their area. A larger ship relieved the *Petrel*, which returned to Gitmo with Knox, who was exonerated for overstepping his authority.

To help keep the peace, the Marines landed at Santiago, and a second expeditionary force was based at Gitmo for a few months, by which time the royalists subdued the rebels.

Conflict then shifted to the base, forcing Knox to turn his persuasive skills on the growing friction among cliques that had developed on the base. He reportedly succeeded in eliminating much of this trouble before he became ill in September of 1917, whereupon the Navy sent him home.

A panoramic view of the Atlantic Fleet, Second Regiment, encamped at Deer

"THE GREAT WAR"

That spring the United States entered into a much bigger war—World War I, which found Gitmo unprepared to meet a wartime emergency. But the war motivated the politicians to grant appropriations to increase fuel oil and water storage and new buildings for fleet activities at Gitmo. Since these weren't finished until the end of the war, Gitmo's principal contribution to the war effort was as a refueling station for ships. Whether or not this had anything to do with the base commandant's frame of mind is unknown. He went insane and had to be relieved of duty in 1920.

For the next twenty years, little happened at Gitmo. The station took on added life with the arrival of the fleet each winter, despite the lack of facilities for entertainment and recreation. Also, Prohibition was in effect. A few miles away, however, Caimanera provided plenty of action: rum, cigars, gambling, and various sorts of not too wholesome entertainment.

Without the fleet, life at Gitmo was quiet. One writer in 1926 described the base as a scene of military personnel doggedly going about their duties despite the persistent heat. Navy wives would ride lazy ponies over McCalla Hill to call on the ladies of the Marine Corps at Fisherman's Point. Chinese coolies tended the boilers of the power plant or pushed tiny flat cars under the scrutiny of a Cuban foreman.

When the *Kittery* arrived with passengers and freight bound for the Caribbean, a dance was held at Caimanera. Four times a week the mail came from Havana by rail.

Although some may find it difficult to believe, life at Gitmo then was even more monotonous than it can be today:

> A shout or a loud, hearty laugh would be as noteworthy in Guantánamo as it would be in a church. There is just enough tennis to keep in condition, just enough swimming to keep moderately cool, just enough bridge of an evening to exhaust the conversation of your neighbors, and an occasional ride up the bay for a cocktail on Pablo's back gallery or a cold bottle of beer in Jim

Point, 1910

Beauzay's or O'Brien's. Even babies seldom break the drowsy routine, for expectant mothers usually hurry back home to the states. . . . Baseball teams spill over the recreation field . . . on Hicacal Beach are hundreds of swimmers. Spring tides roll inches deep over the golfing fairways, and the bare greens are full of crab holes, but you can't expect everything.

One of the most notable improvements in the station at this time was the erection of a distilling plant, which couldn't have been more timely. Only two light showers fell on the station during 1925–1927, creating Gitmo's most serious drought. An increased water supply was also needed in the winter of 1927 when the 210 ships of the Atlantic and Pacific fleets came together for joint maneuvers at Gitmo.

Meanwhile, beneath the placid façade of Gitmo, an ongoing battle split the station into two warring factions over the supply of beef and milk. The dispute involved the propriety of allowing a Cuban, Abelardo Marquez, to have a ranch, slaughterhouse, and grazing lands on the eastern part of the reservation from which he provided beef, veal, and milk for the base. Disgruntled Cubans, particularly prospective competitors, complained that this arrangement violated the 1903 agreement prohibiting private enterprise on the base.

In 1940, the Navy terminated the Marquez lease and gave it and the ranch for two years to a wealthy American landowner who lived nearby in Cuba.

Other civilian houses and shacks, built with materials from scrap piles and other unorthodox sources, cluttered the base. The Navy tolerated the shanties until Captain Thomas L. Johnson took command. Known as the "destroying angel," the severe, unsmiling CO ordered all of the unauthorized buildings torn down.

The Marquez ranch supplied meat and milk.

A few months after the departure of the destroying angel, however, more Cuban civilians poured onto the base, seeking a haven from yet another revolution on the island. In August of 1933, the regime of President Gerardo Machado was overthrown. Financiers, owners of sugar mills, businessmen, and high-ranking Cuban officials escaped assassination by fleeing to Gitmo. United States ships cruised around the Cuban coast in case they were needed to protect North American lives and property. But although Cuban compatriots were slaughtered, North Americans were not molested.

In the quiet years that followed, a survey team recommended the Yateras River as Gitmo's water source. Also noteworthy were the first amphibious maneuvers, involving the Marines and the station ship, which were conducted on one of the outer beaches. On a small scale, this was the initial development of the amphibious techniques later to be tried in war.

Things were so quiet in fact that only two survey ships and a converted yacht were using Gitmo as a coaling station. So in 1938 the Navy closed the coaling operation, leaving only 367 military personnel to run the base.

At the same time, with war threatening in Europe, a survey board recommended that the base be expanded as a naval operating base, to include substantial air facilities for modern warfare. The Government realized that the Caribbean area would be important to the defense of North America if the United States were drawn into the war.

WORLD WAR II

Redesigned as a Naval Operating Base on April 1, 1941, Gitmo's authorities embarked on a huge expansion program costing $34 million.

Thousands of military and civilian personnel were assigned to the base. The civilian influx reached thirteen thousand, an historical peak for this type of personnel.

As was the case during other periods of increase, Gitmo wasn't ready for the newcomers. To cite one example, when the first commander of the new Naval Air Station and his wife arrived at Gitmo, they found that their house, which had been painted that very day, had no sink, ice box, or stove. They borrowed dishes, but couldn't find a can opener. So they used a hammer and nail to open their tins of food. They left their clothes in suitcases and got orange crates from the commissary to use as bedside tables. The lack of furniture, however, simplified house cleaning, which was a constant struggle due to the fine brown dust that blew through the jalousie windows and settled on everything.

It's no wonder that when anything came in at the Ship's Service Store, women bought it whether they needed it or not.

Shopping in the early days

The new residents also had blackouts to contend with. One lasted for two weeks. But like the war, it often brought people together. At night, friends would gather and sing songs in the dark or sit outside and count the stars.

The base, of course, was usually a busy place at that time. The Marines moved from Fisherman's Point to a new self-contained base for two thousand men, located beyond Deer Point. Roads, sewers, telephones, and a power and water treatment plant had to be put in.

In addition to airfields at McCalla Hill and Leeward Point, two outlying airfields were constructed, one at La Verdad and the other at Los Caños. But they had little use; this and the need for constant repair led to their abandonment a year later.

Other projects included dredging of certain areas of the bay, construction of a school and chapel, and imbedding ninety-two magazines throughout the hills. Batteries with three- and six-inch guns were installed in the hills and on the coast.

An experimental Mobile Hospital Unit arrived, the first of its kind, and established a 500-bed hospital among the chaparrel and cactus at Mobile Point. This great innovation in Naval medical history started off in typically military SNAFU fashion. The first materials landed on the dock were caskets and furniture. The first-needed equipment, such as tents, tools, and stoves, were unloaded four days later. Because only a few construction men were assigned to set up the hospital, the chief medical diagnostician became supervisor of tent erection; the psychiatrist devised and installed showers; hospital corpsmen acted as carpenters, machinists, and longshoremen.

In spite of the difficulties, the hospital began operation in two weeks. Eventually, the lessons learned on the coral of Guantánamo saved incalculable lives on the atolls of the Pacific.

144

The Navy's first mobile hospital, an experiment that later saved lives of fighting men in the Pacific during World War II.

In addition to the mammoth construction program, the Navy spent a half million dollars to expand recreational facilities on the base, including twenty tennis courts, six basketball courts, twenty softball fields, three baseball fields, a golf course, three swimming pools, a skeet range, a movie lyceum, and a new officers' club. All of this and Cuba, too: liberty parties were organized to Guantánamo City and Santiago.

The Navy Department picked Gitmo for an experiment in off-duty education after becoming swamped with requests from advanced military bases for help in aiding young servicemen to continue their interrupted education. Following the success of the Gitmo experiment, the Navy rapidly established other overseas educational centers and sent education officers to Gitmo to observe its model educational services.

After initial hardships and inconveniences, Gitmo life became what is described as "pleasant" until war embroiled the United States. Gitmo quickly became the center of the action in the Caribbean, where German subs were wrecking havoc on Allied shipping. The Germans sank 257 ships there in 1942.

The Navy evacuated families from the base and appropriated their houses for bachelor quarters. Their Cuban servants were sent home and their houses occupied in an effort to find housing for all additional servicemen.

The commandant of the base, Rear Admiral G. L. Weyler, took charge of the anti-submarine warfare. The Navy provided Allied ships with air cover, placed them in convoys, and routed them to Gitmo. There, they were formed into new convoys with other vessels going to the same destinations. Gitmo became known as the "Crossroads of the Caribbean." Only New York City handled more ship movement through its port.

During 1944, the number of Allied sinkings in the Caribbean dropped dramatically—to only two ships.

Completed in 1941, the first base school was reorganized after World War II.

Hundreds of military personnel left as the war machine began to grind down.

As had happened before during periods between wars, the future of Gitmo remained in doubt. The government cut back most aspects of Gitmo's operations, but not all. The Shakedown Task Group moved from Bermuda and became what is today's Fleet Training Group. The forerunner of the air squadron arrived from San Juan. And the largest dry dock ever built on inland waters was brought to Gitmo and secured to Pier One.

The end of hostilities also meant that the base was safe again for dependents and civil servants. By January of 1946, the base had once again settled down to its normal routine. The deluge of families, however, forced many changes in the living conditions. By 1948, a total of 1329 women and children resided on the base. The school restarted and a kindergarten was added.

The only threat to the tranquility was fermenting among the 2600 civilian employees, 95 percent of whom were Spanish. They were discontented because the Navy had no uniform policy concerning their pay, promotion, safety, and other aspects of their working situation. The Navy admitted that industrial relations lagged far behind that of the "continental United States" and eventually established a Base Industrial Relations Department.

The first union was created in 1950.

THE KOREAN WAR

The outbreak of the Korean War initiated the fourth major expansion of Gitmo. A new runway and associated facilities for jet aircraft were constructed at Leeward Point, which enjoys better wind conditions than McCalla Field.

Another significant undertaking was the giving of names to the roads on the base, most of which had none until 1951. This had made traveling around the base somewhat of an adventure for new personnel. The roads were called after Americans and Cubans who had some connection with Gitmo; other names derived from the functional uses of the roads, such as Boat Shed Road.

Gitmo itself was changed on June 18, 1952, to a Naval Base. As its Golden Anniversary approached, the base had a population of eleven thousand—eight thousand residents and three thousand Cuban commuters—that didn't include thousands from visiting ships.

The fence line was improved and extended at this time, including that part across the inlet called Grandillo Bay. The Seabees filled in the upper part of the inlet, creating a causeway that joined North Toro Cay to the Windward side of Guantánamo Bay.

Further south, engineers dredged the bay (for the second time in the history of the base) because the larger aircraft carriers and battleships couldn't dock. The big ships had been forced to anchor at the mouth of the bay.

North of the fence, one more Cuban revolution flared. It ignited on March 10, 1952, when former President Batista, with United States support, grabbed control of the government in a surprise coup d'etat. The short, almost bloodless revolt didn't effect the base much, except that liberty was stopped for a few days and asylum was granted for a Cuban naval officer.

But in the Batista takeover, the groundwork was laid for the events that would alter Gitmo life more than any of the wars: the advent of Fidel Castro and the isolation of the base behind the Cactus Curtain.

Appendix B

U.S.-CUBA TREATY AGREEMENT

After the United States forced Spain to grant Cuba independence in 1903, the United States and Cuba signed an agreement allowing the United States to use a 45.4-square-mile parcel of land at Guantánamo Bay. The agreement, which authorized a naval coaling station, was signed by U.S. President Theodore Roosevelt and Cuban President Tomas Estrada Palma.

The original agreement was reaffirmed by a treaty signed in 1934 as part of President Franklin D. Roosevelt's Good Neighbor Policy. The main points concerning the U.S. Naval Base at Guantánamo Bay are:

1. Cuba retains ultimate sovereignty over the area.
2. The United States can lease the area indefinitely. The lease can be voided only by the United States abandoning the area or by mutual agreement of the two countries.
3. The United States cannot expand the area of the base and must maintain boundaries by a well-marked perimeter fence.
4. Commercial, industrial, or private enterprises are not permitted.
5. The base cannot be used as a safe haven for fugitives wanted under Cuban law. Such individuals shall be delivered upon demand to Cuban authorities.
6. No material, merchandise, or munitions are to be transported into Cuban territory.
7. Cuba and its trading partners are guaranteed free access to Cuba through the bay.
8. The United States pays an annual rent of $4,085 for the lease of the base.*
9. The base cannot be used as a port of entry to or exit from Cuba.

*Only one rent check has been cashed since Fidel Castro took over the Cuban Government in 1959. That was in the first full year of his control of Cuba.

Bibliography

Allman, T. D., "Guantánamo: Days of Future Past," *New Times*, September 18, 1978, p. 4+.

"Bases in South America and the Caribbean Area Including Bermuda," *Building the Navy's Bases in World War II: History of the Bureau of Yards and Docks and the Civil Engineer Corps, 1940-1946*, Vols. I & II, United States Government Printing Office, Washington, D.C., 1947.

Bender, Lynn D., "Gitmo—Vestige of Americana in Cuba," *U.S. Naval Institute Proceedings*, July 1968, pp. 128-131.

Bienvenido, revised April 1983, Public Affairs Office, U.S. Naval Base, Guantánamo Bay, Cuba.

Binder, David, "Life is Clean and Healthy but Isolated at U.S. Navy Base in Cuba," *The New York Times*, September 5, 1977.

Cochran, Charles L., "U.S. Treaty Rights in the Caribbean," *U.S. Naval Institute Proceedings*, July 1968, pp. 128-131.

Dudney, R., "With the U.S. Marines at Guantánamo," *U.S. News & World Report*, October 29, 1979, p. 41+.

Halloran, Richard, "Soviet Said to Add Troops in Cuba," *The New York Times*, June 28, 1977.

Handleman, Howard, "Castro: Yankee Go Home," *U.S. News & World Report*, August 27, 1973, pp. 56-8.

History of a Takeover: The US naval base at Guantánamo Bay, Republic of Cuba Ministry of Foregin [sic] Affairs, 1979.

Healy, David F., *The United States in Cuba, 1898-1902*, University of Wisconsin Press, Madison, Wisc., 1963.

Hopkins, Gary, "Big Mission in the Caribbean," *All Hands*, September 1983, pp. 20-30.

Kahn, E. J., Jr., "Reporter at Large: Marines' Landing; Maneuvers at Guantánamo," *New Yorker*, November 12, 1979, p. 190 + .

Koze, David, & Varner, B. D., *The History of Guantánamo Bay*, Third Edition, U.S. Naval Base, Guantánamo Bay, Cuba, 1964.

—"Life on the Rock," *All Hands*, June 1977, pp. 18-19.

Marks, John, "The C.I.A., Cuba and Terrorism," *The New York Times*, June 28, 1977.

Martin, D. C., "On the Rock: Guantánamo," *Newsweek*, October 15, 1979, p. 67.

Miller, T., "Sun Sometimes Sets on the American Empire," *Esquire*, September 1973, p. 101 + .

Murphy, Marion Emerson, *The History of Guantánamo Bay*, second edition, U.S. Naval Base, Guantánamo Bay, Cuba, 1953.

Pomfrey, John, *United States Naval Base, Guantánamo Bay, Cuba, 1964-1982*, Guantánamo Bay Officers' Wives' Club, U.S. Naval Base, Guantánamo Bay, Cuba, September 1982.

Sider, Don, "Good Life at GITMO," *Time*, October 15, 1979, p. 51.

Thomas, Hugh, *Cuba: The Pursuit of Freedom*, Harper & Row, New York, 1971.

Thomas, Jo, "Invaders, Guantánamo Bound, Come Only to Grief," *New York Times*, September 7, 1981.

—"Time Running Out for Cuban Commuters," *U.S. News & World Report*, August 13, 1973, p. 81.

Wheeler, Dan, "Island on an Island," *All Hands*, June 1977, pp. 12-16.

Wilkes, Jr., Paul D., "The 81-day Wonder," *All Hands*, March 1980, pp. 24-27.

Index

AFRTS (Armed Forces Radio and Television Service), 33, 50, 55-58
DEFEX broadcasting, 80-82, 85
live shows, 72-75
news, 61 f, 73 f
personnel, 71 f, 79, 111
programming, 58 f, 80
radio, AM, FM, 58
satellite use, 58
television, 58 ff
Aircraft. See individual models.
Aircraft carriers, 114-24, 147
Air Force, U.S., 35
Alaskan Forces Satellite Network, 58
Alcohol. See Drinking.
AM radio. See AFRTS, radio.
Animals, 88, 103, 133
Anti-submarine warfare, 145
Architecture. See Housing.
Armed Forces Radio and Television Service. See AFRTS.
Athletics. See Sports.
Atlantic Fleet, 114
Automobiles, 42. See also Gitmo Specials, Traffic regulations.
Auto repair shop, 42

Ballistic missiles. See Missiles.
Barcelona, Spain, 99
Barracks. See Housing.
Barracuda, 70, 104
Barrel Boat, 107 f
Barrel Club, 108
Barrier road, 89
Batista, Fulgencio, 14, 95, 147
Bay Hill Barracks, 46-48
Bay of Pigs invasion, 15 f, 19, 106
Bed check, 47
Blockade, U.S., 17. See also U.S.-Castro relations.
Blue Caribe, 75
Boats. See also individual ships, Recreation.
Boat shed, 81
Boat Shed Road, 147
Boquerón, 19, 93, 107
Boundary. See Fence line.
Bounty, H.M.S., 81
Boxer, U.S.S., 91
Boy Scouts, 104
Brahmans. See Cattle.
Britain, 130 f
Bulkeley, John D., 20 f, 99
Bulkeley, Mrs. John D., 22
Bulkeley Hill, 20 f, 87, 110
Bureau of Naval Personnel, 33

C-141, 69
C-130, 69
Cactus. *See* Vegetation, Fence line.
Cactus Curtain, 12, 16, 82, 89. *See also* Fence line.
Caimanera, 19, 93, 98, 131 f, 134, 138, 141
Cars. *See* Transportation, Gitmo Specials.
Carter, Jimmy, 27, 82
Caravella Point, 54
Castro, Fidel. *See also* Commuters, U.S.-Castro relations.
   anti-treaty arguments, 25-29
   attempted assassination of, 15
   confiscates U.S. property, 15
   cuts Gitmo electricity, 23
   involvement in Latin America, 14, 26
   orders U.S. Embassy reduction, 15
   refuses to cash rent checks, 18, 148
   relations with U.S., 14-32
   stops commuter hiring, 15, 96
   Soviet Union support of, 13 f, 26
   turns off Gitmo water, 19, 99
Castro, Raúl, 14
Cattle, 88 f, 94
Cattle Car, 52
Cattle Chute, 12, 93 f
Cayo del Toro, 132, 134
Central Intelligence Agency, 15 f
Channel 8. *See* AFRTS.
Chapel, 144
Charlie Brown, 39. *See also* Ferries.
Chinese labor, 141
CIA. *See* Central Intelligence Agency.
Climate, 37 f, 87
   hurricanes, 43, 48, 84 f

rain, 17, 37, 142
Clubs, 101 f, 108, 145
CO. *See* Commanding officer.
Coast Guard, U.S., 30, 40
Coffee shop. *See* Navy Exchange coffee shop.
Columbus, 37, 130
Commandant Hill, 49
Commanding officer, 63, 84
Command Quiz, 59, 74
Commissary, 44, 94. *See also* Shopping.
Communications, 63-65, 132, 134
Communications satellite facility, 64
Community center. *See* Morin Center.
Commuters
   affected by Cuban revolution, 14, 95 f
   affected by U.S.-Castro relations, 15, 92-94
   attrition of, 96
   Castro gain from, 95
   daily routine, 11 f, 93 f
   hiring stopped, 15, 95
   industrial relations, 146
   job benefits, 94 f
   search of, 11, 92-94
   U.S. gain from, 94 f
Congressional Medal of Honor, 55, 133
Congressional visit, 77, 85-87
Construction. *See* Housing.
Cooking with the Commander, 74, 112
Cooper Field, 52
Coral, 104 f
Corinasco Cove, 138
Corpsmen, 54
Crane, Stephen, 133
Crime, 45 f

154

Marine Corps, (continued)
   harassed by Cuban sentries, 20 f
   minefield maintenance, 11, 91
   Navy adversaries, 110 f
   reinforcing units, 82-84
   in Spanish-American War, 132-34
Marquez, Abelardo, 142
MARS. See Military affiliate radio
   system.
Master-at-arms, 47
   barracks, 47
   dining hall, 85
MAU (Marine Amphibious Unit).
   See Marine Corps amphibi-
   ous operations.
McCalla Field, 146
McCalla Hill, 41, 132, 141, 144
McGovern, George, 25
McKinley, William, 132
Mechanical cow, 69
Mess hall. See Dining facilities.
Miami, Florida, 46, 48, 102, 106
MIG, 26, 35, 38
Military affiliate radio system, 64
Military Airlift Command, 34, 38
Military exercises, 81. See also
   Defense Mobilization Ex-
   ercise.
Mines
   Cuban, 90
   in Spanish-American War, 134
   simulated in training, 117
   U.S., 11, 90 f
Mini-mart, 39, 69 f
Missile Crisis, 11, 16-19, 31 f, 96
Missiles, 16-18. See also Missile
   Crisis.
Mobile canteen. See Navy Ex-
   change Mobile Canteen.
Mobile Hospital Unit, 144
Mobile Point, 144
Mobilization. See Defense Mobili-
   zation Exercise.

Morin, William H., 55
Morin Center, 55-57, 75
Mount Vernon, 130
Movie censorship, 77
Movies. See Entertainment, Ly-
   ceums.

National Security Agency, 61
Naval Air Station. See Leeward
   Point.
Naval Cemetery, 139
Naval Photographic Center, 129
Naval Schools of Photography, 117
Navy Exchange, 12, 37, 39, 69, 94,
   100. See also individual ser-
   vices.
Navy Exchange coffee shop, 71,
   86
Navy Exchange Mobile Canteen,
   53
Navy Lodge, 49
Newsmen. See Journalists.
Nicaragua, 27
Nixon, Richard, 25, 106
No-man's-land, 12. See also Fence
   line.
Norfolk, Virginia, 30, 34, 45, 102,
   108
North Toro Cay, 136, 147
Northeast Gate, 12, 21, 23, 87-94,
   99
Noticías en Español, 74
November Company, 78 f
Nurses, 18, 54

Ocean Venture, 83 f
Old Dominion University, 102
Oriente Province, 37, 138

Palma, Estrada, 136, 148
Palm trees. See Vegetation.

About the Author

Theodore K. Mason served as Armed Forces Television supervisor during a tour of duty at the United States Naval Base, Guantánamo Bay, Cuba.

Born in California, he was raised in Klamath Falls, Oregon, and attended the University of Oregon. After graduating with a Bachelor of Arts degree in English, he spent five years in the Navy.

He has lived in New Zealand and also in Australia, where his first book was published and he taught high school for two years.

New York City is currently his home.